Gilles Anouil

THE POOR are the Church

A Conversation with **Fr. Joseph Wresinski,** *Founder of* the **Fourth World Movement**

D1416340

TWENTY-THIRD PUBLICATIONS
185 Willow Street • PO BOX 180 • MYSTIC, CT 06355
TEL: 1-800-321-0411 • FAX: 1-800-572-0788
E-MAIL: ttpubs@aol.com • www.twentythirdpublications.com

Dedication

To Alwine de Vos van Steenwijk
to the Permanent Volunteers of
ATD Fourth World Movement
to all my companions on the way
to the Fourth World families
who have convinced me that
the poor are the church

Translated from the French by Mary Rabagliati, Fanchette Clement-Fanelli, Monsignor Winus Roeten, and Sister Fara Impastato with the assistance of Charles Courtney, Geneviève Defraigne Tardieu, Paula Ross, and Moya Amateau. Endnotes by Monsignor Winus Roeten and Sister Fara Impastato.

Original title: Les pauvres sont l'Eglise
Originally Published: ISBN 2227 32032x
© Copyright Editions du Centurion, Paris, 1983.

Twenty-Third Publications
A Division of Bayard
185 Willow Street
P.O. Box 180
Mystic, CT 06355
(860) 536-2611
(800) 321-0411
www.twentythirdpublications.com

ISBN:1-58595-183-8
Library of Congress Catalog Card Number: 2001135543
Printed in the U.S.A.

"Meeting Joseph Wresinski changed my life. This book is your chance to meet the man and his vision. Wresinski presents the Fourth World (those in extreme poverty) as at once our mirror and our hope. If destination is not the opposite of grace but the occasion for it, then the poor and the rejected are us. The poor are the church, and we are fully in the church only when we stand with the poorest. If you choose to read this book, be prepared to be changed."

Charles Courtney
Professor of Philosophy of Religion,
Drew University

"The Fourth World Movement is an inspiration to all who care about the poor. In *The Poor Are the Church*, we are inspired by Father Wresinski, who explains to us how his love for the church and his love for the poor came together in his work and the work of those who follow him in the Fourth World."

Mary Jo Bane
Kennedy School of Government,
Harvard University

"The title is radical—*The Poor Are the Church*. At first, one assumes that he must mean that the church must care about the poor or that the poor must be included in the church; but, in fact, Father Wresinski argues biblically, experientially, and compellingly that the church has no existence, much less authenticity, apart from the poor. It is a belief that has guided the extraordinary, asset-focused, culturally-sensitive, and empowering work of the Fourth World Movement. This book gives us deeper insights into the reasons for and implications of that belief. I look forward, as I believe every reader will, to applying those insights to the task of working with and for high-risk youth and their families, in America and around the world."

Rev. Ray Hammond
Cofounder, Ten Point Coalition

Table of Contents

Preface

Twelve years ago, one of the best students in a small seminar I was directing at the School of Political Sciences asked me to help him find an opening in journalism, my profession, once he had passed his finals. Thanks to a friend, I succeeded in getting him into a training course at a large international press agency, and I quickly called to tell him the good news. "Thank you for your help," he replied, "but I have decided to follow another career: I am going to work in shantytowns." "Well done! How generous! Will this be with people from the Maghreb, with Africans, or some other immigrant group?" I asked him. "Not at all," he told me. "With French people like you and me. There are thousands, literally hundreds of thousands of them."

I still remember my astonishment at the time. Being a journalist and curious, I wanted to know more. That was how I came into contact with Father Joseph Wresinski and his Fourth World Movement.[1] I discovered the world of the disadvantaged right at our doorstep, a world we have ignored for generations. While my student became a full-time volunteer for the Fourth World Movement, I attempted to offer my humble services as an "ally," one who participates in the Movement as a supporter on a part-time basis.[2]

Then, one day, in an effort to optimally contribute to this project, I proposed to Father Joseph that I use my skill as a journalist to compile a book of interviews with him. After much thought, he agreed. This is typical of him. I shall always remember those many hours spent in Pierrelaye, mostly on Saturday mornings. I shall remember his replies, both restrained and impassioned; his watchful eyes; and his round face, affectionate and determined. "Do you think all this is of any interest?" he often asked me after our sessions. I, myself, never worried about this, nor do I worry now. It is up to the readers to judge. Anyhow, "interest" is a word far too weak to describe the power of Father Joseph's basic message.

Unfortunately, I was not able to finish the project because my new job sent me to the other side of the world. Accustomed to making up for the shortcomings of well-intentioned, fickle characters like me, Father Joseph finished the text himself, with the help of Alwine de Vos van Steenwijk.

I am infinitely grateful to him for agreeing to undertake this dialogue, which was not really between him and me but between him and every person who reads this book.

—Gilles Anouil

Preface to the English Edition

Americans have typically thought of poverty in two distinct ways. Most commonly, poverty has been diagnosed as some type of deficiency at the individual or family level—a deficiency in income or wealth, a deficiency in skills or education, or simply a general lack of resources. Persons on the Right, in particular, have often argued that the poor are so because they are deficient in moral rectitude. These different diagnoses imply different policies for ameliorating the situation of the poor—income transfers, job training and educational programs, or punishment for deviant behavior. However, as different as these diagnoses are, they share a common perspective. They all see the problem of poverty as existing in specific individuals or in families. Individuals and families are poor because they have specific characteristics that cause them to fail in their pursuit of social and economic success.

A more radical position espoused by the Left has been that poverty is structural. Individuals are poor because they are oppressed by those in power. In the classic Marxist perspective, the poor provide the surplus labor that is necessary for capitalism to function. In the case of blacks and other minorities, they are disproportionately poor because of racism and discrimination. In sharp contrast to the deficiency perspective, poverty exists not in the individual, but as a consequence of an inegalitarian economy and social system.

Although the deficit and the structural understandings of poverty are quite different, they both see poverty and the poor as problems that are "out there." The question *The Poor Are the Church* asks is whether these two understandings, either separately or together, are adequate for fully grasping the problem of poverty. In the interviews with Gilles Anouil contained in this book, Father Joseph Wresinski, the founder of the Fourth World Movement, emphatically states that the answer is no.

The Poor Are the Church is a very Christian and specifically Catholic book. It tells us that we can only appreciate Christ if we fully understand him in terms of his decision to live as one of the poor. In declaring that the poor are the Church, Wresinski tells us that whenever the Church is understood as separate from the poor, it is no longer truly the Church. Thus, our alienation from God stems directly from our failure to be in communion with the poor— to share in their suffering, to understand that their plight is ours, or more basically, to understand that the poor are "us." God is always with the poor. If we fail to be united with the poor, then we fail in our relationship with God.

What does this all mean for a Jew like myself or even more generally to a nonbeliever? Is this only a book for Catholics? In a *Boston Globe* column (April 10, 2001), renowned author and former Catholic priest James Carroll talks about the currently popular idea of compassion in ways that are quite consistent with Wresinski's thinking. Carroll's message is to individuals of all faiths. He points out that compassion means to suffer with. It is distinct from pity. Pity is experienced at a distance and is offered "from above." To pity the poor is to see them as lamentable and without full dignity. Pity divides the world into rescuers and victims; in doing so it maintains the inherent inequality between the two. Pity is often more beneficial to the one who offers it than to the one who receives it.

Carroll argues that compassion involves suffering with the poor on equal terms. Furthermore, it implies that changes must take place in our partnership with the poor; that what should determine the extent of change is not what we are capable of or willing to give, but rather what the poor require. When we are compassionate, we put ourselves in a position of equality with the poor. In doing so, we understand that they and we are, to use a term from political philosophy, within the same moral sphere. This is what I take to be the core message of *The Poor Are the Church*. When we see ourselves and the poor as living distinct lives, as existing within separate moral spheres, it is our moral perspective that is flawed.

How does our failure to understand that the poor are "us," a failure of true compassion, matter? Compassion is critical if we are to be in correct relation to the poor. If we are only concerned with poverty in terms of attempting to improve the poor's deficiencies (on whatever level), we seriously risk seeing ourselves as their superiors. We are the givers, they are the takers. We engage in noblesse oblige. In helping the poor we assert our own moral worth, while potentially depreciating the moral dignity of those whom we intend to help.

If we address poverty as a problem of structural inequity or political injustice, there is the risk that we believe that others, but not ourselves, are responsible for the situation of the poor. Moral hubris becomes a distinct possibility. This is one of the two key problems that Wresinski sees in leftist revolutionary movements. Wresinski is quick to point out that God is equally present in the rich and the poor. The moral status of the poor should not be exalted by demonizing the rich. Wresinski also believes that revolutions almost never truly aid the poor. Rather, they benefit the revolutionaries.

If one merely skims through *The Poor Are the Church*, it is easy to believe that the poor Wresinski speaks of—those in extreme poverty, the social excluded—are both impoverished and docile. They live simple lives of misery. Like wretched, abandoned puppies, they are individuals for whom we should feel sympathy. This is a serious misunderstanding of Wresinski! At several points Wresinski notes that he ended up in fist fights with the very poor with whom he worked and lived. Domestic abuse among the poor is a widespread problem. These are individuals who live profoundly difficult lives and who, as a result, can be very difficult to live with.

In American terms, Wresinski's poor, at least by some definitions, is what has come to be known as the underclass. After the uproar caused by the Moynihan Report in 1965 and its concern with the increasing number of African-American children being born out of wedlock, it became politically incorrect for academics on the Left to discuss, much less analyze, behavioral issues among the poor. Any attempt to do so was seen as "blaming the victim."

The publication of William Julius Wilson's *The Truly Disadvantaged* in 1987, changed this. Wilson rebuked the attack on the Moynihan Report and its concern with single parent households. Whereas Moynihan was concerned that the percentage of African-American children being born out of wedlock was approaching thirty percent, two decades later it was nearly seventy percent. Wilson argued that poverty was not simply a matter of economic impoverishment but also a problem of out-of-wedlock childbearing, long-term unemployment, welfare dependency, and crime. In short, deviant behavior was an issue. The term "underclass," however, is currently in disrepute. It is now generally seen as a derogatory term that demonizes the poor (for example, see Michael Katz's *The Underclass Controversy*). In terms of the above discussion, the term underclass is viewed as implying that the poor are morally deficient and thus lack full human dignity. In Katz's terms, it results in our seeing the poor as "the other."

Certainly one of the most powerful accomplishments of Fr. Wresinski is his ability to recognize how problematic the lives of those in extreme poverty are, his so-called Fourth World, while simultaneously asserting their full human dignity. In places he even suggests that the dignity of the poor surpasses our own.

How can we recognize how problematic the lives of Fourth World persons are without seeing them as "the other"? We do this by seeing ourselves as one with the poor. For Fr. Wresinski and so many Fourth World workers, this has meant living with and being one of the poor. The poor person is like that difficult and constantly disruptive family member who has never succeeded in life. It is that son or daughter, brother or sister or parent, whom the family is always tempted to disown. However, if we truly understand that this individual is a member of our family, then we know that we are obligated to accept him or her as such. Wresinski's argument, although he does not specifically use this analogy, is that we have, in fact, disowned the poor. For our own moral integrity we need to reown them and allow them to own us.

Wresinski's argument is that of an iconoclast. He suggests that as long as we see the poor as people "out there"—either as a result of some form of deficiency or as the result of structural oppression by others—we can never truly deal with those in extreme poverty, the Fourth World. Only by understanding that those in the Fourth World are our moral equals and by embracing them as full members of society—neighbors, friends—can we possibly begin to deal with the problem of extreme poverty. This is a radical proposal. It suggests that giving charity, paying higher taxes, voting correctly, and political advocacy are not nearly enough. It is only by fundamentally changing our relationship to the poor that true change will be possible.

Wresinski's position is also philosophically radical. It is a rejection of the traditional enlightenment/liberal conception of the self as the wholly atomistic individual. Seen from this latter perspective the poor are unsuccessful individuals (or families), perhaps because of their own deficiencies or because of the unjust actions of others. In either case, poverty is reduced by changing their situation.

In Wresinski's analysis poverty represents the failure of society. The poor are simply (and tragically) the ones forced to bear most directly the costs of this failure. In important respects, Wresinski's analysis rests on a communitarian theory of poverty. Communitarianism, in contrast to traditional philosophical liberalism, defines the self not as an autonomous entity but by the nexus of relations in which an individual is embedded. As a result, individuals are poor not because of their particular circumstances but because of their relation, or lack thereof, to others in society. Those in extreme poverty, the socially excluded, are such because they are related to as "the other."

Let me make this more concrete by describing a specific example. Former neo-conservative economist Glenn Loury often talks about the tragedy of so many young black males in America who have been given extended terms in jail for minor drug offenses. Loury does not want to simply let all these individuals out of jail. They have committed crimes. What he is appalled by is society's comfort with the status quo. He argues that if these were the children of white middle-class families, these high levels of incarceration would never be tolerated. We, as a society, would search for alternative solutions. It is precisely because we see young black youth as "the other" that it is politically acceptable to deal with their involvement in drugs through imprisonment.

Wresinski understands the situation of the poor from a deeply Catholic perspective. His message, however, is not just for Catholics but for us all. He calls us to understand poverty in a profoundly different way, not just as destitution and oppression but as social isolation. This isolation is created by us all to the degree that we live apart from the poor and fail to understand that their fate is ours.

In Judaism, those in extreme poverty, the socially isolated, are described as "the stranger." The great Jewish medieval sage Maimonides, in the Mishneh Torah, his systematic presentation of Jewish law, states (Law of Virtue 6:3-4):

> To love the stranger who comes to take refuge beneath the wings of the Shekinah (God) is the fulfillment of two positive precepts. First, because he is included among neighbors (whom we are committed to love). And secondly, because he is a stranger, and the Torah said, "Love you therefore the stranger" (Deut 10:19). God charged (us) concerning the love of the stranger, even as He charged us concerning love of Himself, as it is said, "You shall love the Lord our God" (ibid. 6:5). The Holy One, blessed be He, loves strangers, as it is said, "And He loves the stranger" (ibid. 10:18).

It would seem that Wresinski and Maimonides are in strong agreement about what God requires of us with respect to the poor.

—Christopher Winship,
Professor of Sociology, Harvard University
June 2001

Introduction

An Encounter with Father Joseph[3]

As soon as we started reading these dialogues between Father Joseph Wresinski and Gilles Anouil, we realized it was a gripping book, an account in sync with everyone's deepest convictions. Father Joseph went straight to the essential points, leaving the autobiographical details and the chronicle of the Fourth World Movement to the end. Those who have met him even once know that this man, the founder and leader of the Fourth World Movement, has one main concern—to bear witness to the Church of the poor. Not the Church on the one hand and the poor on the other, but the Church and the poor as one, indissoluble. One word includes the other.

A paradox? This is our first impression because our memories are so full of hackneyed notions about the Church's collusion with the rich and the powerful and its betrayal of the poor. Is this impression justified? We are not concerned with that here. Father Joseph presents another vision: the Church is the Church of the poor; the Church is the poor, and there is no other Church. This is its deepest reality—both legitimately and effectively—its vocation, its raison d'être, and its nature.

Father Joseph speaks about this Church from experience, an experience he can trace back to his childhood. He speaks in an unaffected and straightforward way, without being over-emphatic. He speaks at once of the poor and excluded, of their wretched lives, their destitution, and their shame; and of the Fourth World, a term coined by Father Joseph himself and which has come into everyday use. His words are challenging and disturbing; they reverse the images, representations, and feelings we have concerning the Church and Christianity. Yet there are, in fact, numerous biblical and historical witnesses to this message: Mary, in her Magnificat, Francis of Assisi, Vincent de Paul, Jeanne Jugan, and Charles de Foucauld, to cite only a few. It is the Church of the Gospel, the Church of Jesus that Father Joseph shows us.

Despite the power of Father's Joseph's message, when it came to preparing the interviews for publication, we were beset by the usual preoccupations of editors and wanted to reorganize the material. We wanted to put Father Joseph's biographical account and the chronicle of the Fourth World

Movement at the beginning of the book. After all, narratives would be more likely to satisfy the reader's supposed curiosity. So we wished to switch some chapters around. We discovered, however, that in so doing we would have distorted Father Joseph's very vision. We would have had to present his message as a composite of secondary ideas that followed the event. The essential points of his thought would have been ranked among the additional explanatory remarks. But the intuitions or message are the light, the force, and the cause from which the action springs. They have to come first. Therefore, they have to come first in the book, too. Fortunately, our editorial work left them in their rightful place. All we needed, then, as an introduction was a brief outline of the Movement. A thumbnail description would also have distorted what was to come. So I suggested to Father Joseph an initial conversation outlining his plan in a few words.

One morning he came to our publishing house. I had carefully prepared a few questions, but in fact no questions were necessary. Calmly and directly, Father Joseph gave me an account so enlightening and extensive that I had to transcribe it word for word. A few days later Father Joseph sent me another text: notes recalling his childhood, his mother, and his birth into the Church of the Fourth World.

Father Joseph was in no way self-indulgent in talking about himself; he was relating what he was given to live, discover, and do, as if his role had only been minor, his prophetic acts just the natural and inevitable outcome of circumstances and divine action. He was not trying to gain attention; he wanted to share a vision, an obsession, a plan, and a vocation as if these things did not belong to him alone. Listening to Father Joseph and others like him, you would think they have achieved practically nothing themselves; they almost apologize for being at the crossroads of an outpouring of light and charity, at the outposts of humanity's struggle. They just happened to be there; to encounter reality; to be impelled by this reality to react, invent, act, and love their brothers and sisters "for real." They were encouraged by an invisible and irresistible force. They were "passive" people—a blessed passivity that does not imply indifference but accessibility, availability, vulnerability, and readiness to welcome others and to receive God's active grace. They were divinely inspired to carry a heavy burden, to "support" and to "suffer," which are etymologically the same word; a "passivity"—which is a "passion" in both senses of the word—of being affected within oneself and committing oneself totally. The surprising and determined action of the just springs from this passivity and passion.

And so, to better introduce the book, we print below Father Joseph's own account of his childhood and of the intuitions that are the basis of the Fourth World Movement.

—Charles Ehlinger

A young boy caught in the vicious circle of violence
Fr. Joseph Wresinski

My earliest childhood memories are of a large hospital ward and of my mother shouting at the nun who was supervising us. As a young boy I suffered from rickets, and I had been hospitalized to have my legs straightened.

That day I told my mother that the nun had not let me receive my parcel the previous Sunday. My mother, who obviously had tried hard to gather a few treats, lost her temper. Immediately she wrenched me from the hands of the nuns and brought me back home.

My legs have remained bowed ever since. Throughout my childhood, and especially as a teenager, I was subjected to the ridicule and teasing brought on by this handicap—and endured the added embarrassment of a slight limp.

And so, my first memory of contact with other people was one of injustice and prejudice; these were to leave their mark for the rest of my life. This probably also explains my intolerance to runny noses, crooked legs, and the young bodies—already marred—that surround me now in emergency housing, in hovels, and in slums.

My mother's shouting at the nun did not surprise me. I was used to shouting. At home, my father shouted all the time. He would beat my older brother, much to my mother's despair, as it was always my brother's head that bore the brunt of it. My father frequently cursed my mother, and we lived continually in fear.

It was only much later, when I was a grown man sharing the life of other men like my father and of other families like our own, that I understood my father was a humiliated man. He suffered because he felt he had failed in life; he was ashamed not to be able to give his family security and happiness.

This is the true consequence of extreme poverty. A person cannot live such a humiliating life without reacting. The poor react in the same violent way, nowadays as well as in the past.

Violence was the way of reacting to everyday difficulties of all kinds. Without my realizing it, violence was becoming—for myself and for my father—the means of washing away the numerous humiliations inflicted upon us by extreme poverty.

It still amazes me, after all these years, that my parents talked only about money. The very people who had no money would forever be arguing because of it. When some money did come into the household, they quarreled about what to spend it on.

Later, when my mother was on her own, she would still frequently talk to us about money. And when she talked about the people we associated with, it was always to say they were rich. To her, the parish priests were rich. Even the woman who ran a small neighborhood grocery store was a rich woman in her eyes. My mother was not jealous, but when a person is hungry and in need, the sole focus of attention is on what fulfills the need. This is still true today; and in the poor areas around our cities and towns, exchanges and quarrels always seem to focus on money.

I was committed to the fight for food at a very young age. When I was four years old, I was the one who led our goat to the lower meadows. This goat fed all of us children, including my newborn sister. When I took the goat, I would pass the big gate of the Good Shepherd Convent, where a nun would sometimes chat with me. One day she asked me whether I would serve Mass every morning. That day I became employed for the first time; and it was real employment as far as I was concerned. In return for serving Mass, I would be entitled to a big bowl of coffee with milk, as well as bread and jam and—on holy days—butter. In addition, I would be given two francs a week. It was those two francs that motivated me to take the job.

So, I began to support my family before the age of five. Every morning for almost eleven years, my mother called me for the seven o'clock Mass. It took me at least ten minutes to run to the chapel behind the big walls of the convent. In the winter I was cold and frightened of the dark. Whether it was windy or rainy, I walked along the wide Saint-Jacques Street, almost bent over double, half asleep, sometimes shouting with rage. Then I went down Brault Street, which was deserted and hostile, toward the meadows. I would go and serve Mass for the sisters so I could bring forty sous home to Mother. I don't think I ever missed a single one of those morning duties, and it still seems that my whole childhood revolved around them.

Mother must have been greatly in need when it came to feeding us, to accept sending such a young boy out onto the streets every day. I must also have been aware of her feeling of helplessness, when I took on this duty without bitterness or anger against God.

Shortly after Mass each day I had to repeat the journey at midday. As we were the poorest people in the area, there was nothing unusual about the fact that, on leaving school, I would rush out to the convent again, this time to collect in empty tins a meal made up of leftover food. The Madeleine sisters gave us split peas, lentils, potatoes, and sometimes a few pieces of meat, plus the huge loaf that was our staple diet at family meals.

So, every day of my childhood was influenced by the life, the prayers, and the food offered by the sisters of Good Shepherd convent. It meant we did not go hungry.

I sometimes think of this now when I see children climbing onto rubbish heaps or following their father's cart on the way to clear out some cellar or attic. They pick through the garbage; they salvage metal. I used to serve Mass and wait for our food at the convent door. As in the past, destitute children have no childhood; responsibilities are given to them as soon as they can walk.

They were times, however, when like the poor children of today, I used to play and laugh. I probably used to create my own secret corners, my hiding places, and my exploratory routes in the old part of Angers, where I would build imaginary labyrinths with my friends. However, I had to follow the convent route every day, the path of shame of my childhood, which has wiped from my memory anything that might have been a consolation.

There were other paths of shame also linked to the gnawing need for food. I can picture myself as a small boy, taking back to the grocer's a bottle of walnut oil bought for 50 centimes. If it was not filled right to the cork, Mother would send me back to have a few drops added. It is a never-ending, humiliating struggle for the poor to satisfy their hunger.

Later on, pieces of horsemeat that were too tough had to be taken back to the butcher's. At that time I was seven and had found another job running errands for Marie-Louise, the butcher, who in return would give me the equivalent of two francs' worth of horsemeat every day. Mother would insist that the meat be fresh and tender. She did not hesitate to send me back, if need be, to demand better quality for the family table.

Despite our shame, however, we were strong, and I would unthinkingly pounce on other boys because of the oppressive burden of supporting my family. I remember, at the age of six, beating up a young adversary and leaving him in the hedge. When my mother went to see the nun from kindergarten to find out if I could start elementary school, the nun agreed readily. "Of course," she said, "send him there. He beats up everyone here."

Financial hardship, shame, and violence were all linked together from early childhood.

I do not remember ever coming home from school and finding my mother happy at home. A deserted wife, she never got over the fact that she had to support four children on her own. Then there was talk about my father, especially about the money he was supposed to send, which never came. The gas bills to be paid, the coal needed for the winter, the stove to be replaced....

It was nearly always cold at our house. The former ironworks we lived in was full of draughts. The air would penetrate at the top of the doors and through the partitions. One of these partitions was made of crates covered in wrapping paper. When the paper split, the wind would whip us.

The other reason for the cold was that all the apartments above ours were linked via a common chimney. The stack was often blocked, and when we built a fire, the tailor's daughter, Thérèse, would come down to swear at my mother because Thérèse's apartment was filling with smoke. To avoid conflict, Mother would take from the stove the pieces of coal we had brought from the gasworks' slag heaps—pieces of coal we had taken so much trouble to find and which, because of their poor quality, seemed to accentuate rather than combat the cold that prevailed in the house.

My mother's passivity was similar to that of so many poor mothers whom I meet in destitute areas. Her anxiety about upsetting neighbors stemmed partly from fatigue but more so from fear. Mother was always conscious of being a foreigner, and her fear of being sent back to Spain was very real. She was terrified of the police coming to arrest us for God knows what reason, just like the mothers in emergency housing who are constantly afraid of people coming to do them harm.

I was still quite young the day I confronted Thérèse when she came and insulted Mother about the smoke. I took a poker and brandished it in front of her, shouting. I do not remember what I said in my fit of rage, but after that day our meager fire was allowed to smolder in our old stove with its cracked hearth, which we were always mending with clay we brought from the nearby meadows.

My mother would often complain to others about her torments, about me, and about the worries I caused her, such as my poor progress at school and my bed-wetting. The whole neighborhood knew about it, which added to my shame. The poor do not hide their wounds. They have no strength left to mask the problems of an existence that exhausts them.

However, it was thanks to my mother that I was able to take the exam for the certificate of graduation from primary school. There were very few of us in the independent Catholic school who did not pay tuition, and we were at the bottom of the class. The principal did not want to risk having me as a candidate. He had not let my eldest brother take the exam, and my mother had not objected. However, when my turn came, she did not resign herself so easily. She knew I was not stupid. She knew I had too much responsibility on my shoulders; that I suffered too much and had too deep a perception of injustice. For those of us who received charity, but never all that was due us, injustice was our daily fate. My mother did not want an additional injustice to be done to me. It was she who registered me for the exam.

Only today do I understand the reserves of indignation and courage my mother needed to defend her children. She obstinately defended me again when the charity ladies of the parish conceived the idea of placing me in the orphanage at Auteuil. The plan was reasonable but very humiliating, both for children born in poverty and for their mothers, since poor children were raised separately from other children. In one of those sudden bursts of dignity so characteristic of her, my mother refused. She preferred to give up receiving any charity from this parish.

Yet we were already excluded. Being poor, we were set apart from other people in this lower-middle-class neighborhood, linked to them through charity and not through friendship.

We were not the only ones. I remember a woman who was often drunk, and her illegitimate son. When her son came home in the evening, he used to find his mother lying in the kitchen. He would have to drag her to her bed. He would sometimes come to us, and Mother would invite him to share our bread and soup.

Then there was the fortune teller. She did not want dogs to stop beneath her window. We children used her wall as a urinal, and she hurled abuse at us. We liked her and that was why we annoyed her. We would not have annoyed Rétif the butcher or Cesbron the carpenter. They were the important people of the district; they were not of our world.

One day the fortune teller was found dead from starvation in her slum. For two weeks no one had visited her. That evening Mother cried because the same thing could have happened to us. "Who would care about us?" she said. "That's how I will die."

Was it through my mother that I learned to fight, not as a means to avenge humiliation but to free an excluded people?

One day, one of the oldest boys in the school—his name was Siché—

became furious with a puny boy. He drove him back against a wall in the bathroom and punched and kicked him. Something happened in me. I threw myself at Siché, and now it was my turn to kick and punch. I scratched his face until a teacher came and removed me by force.

Why had I done this? That puny boy was nothing to me. What was I doing defending him? It is that boy, however, who remains in my memory, not the punishment I brought upon myself. I was expelled from school, but everything that happened after the fight remains a blur. What I do remember as a turning point was this boy being beaten up by Siché, who was so much stronger than he was. It seems to me that this fight was the beginning of a struggle in which, although I might be the loser, I would be involved obstinately for the rest of my life.

Joining in the struggle for the excluded is not that simple, however. A person does not become an activist on behalf of individuals scattered here and there: a drunk mother, a fortune teller, or a puny boy. I had to encounter them as one people and to discover I was one of them. As an adult, I had to find myself again in the boys who live in the slum housing surrounding our towns and in the unemployed young people who cry with rage. They perpetuate the memory of my miserable childhood, and they remind me that these people in rags have always existed.

It is within our power to stop this never-ending situation. Extreme poverty will not exist in the future if we accept the task of helping these young people gain awareness of their people; help them transform their violence into a lucid struggle; help them arm themselves with love, hope, and knowledge in order to bring to a close the fight against ignorance, hunger, hand-outs, and exclusion.

This work cannot be merely a government matter; it is also a matter of people wanting to walk alongside those who are excluded and to link their own lives with theirs, sometimes at the cost of leaving everything behind in order to share their fate.

We had only ourselves to offer[4]

We are not creators. We are heirs. In the contemporary Church, other persons in France and various parts of the world started movements as they met the poor and the excluded. Persons such as Abbé Godin, Father Depierre, and Abbé Pierre opened doors and entered the world of the destitute. We are part of a spiritual current—with intelligence guided more by the heart than by ideas—meeting the very poor. Ours is a movement striving for peace, struggling for food, and fighting for justice. Our struggle and our action converge somewhere in our concern for those most despised. We are not creators, although poverty leads us to be inventive; perhaps we are innovators.

Where does our originality lie? At the time when the Fourth World Movement was started, society was confident; everybody thought that progress coupled with aid was going to abolish poverty; nobody questioned this outcome. In such a context, how was it possible at any level of society to believe what we said about poverty? This was the major problem we faced. It was in this context that Abbé Pierre revealed the plight of the poorest and the Fourth World Movement focused on the poorest people as families. This was a bold step, when society was beginning to lose interest in the family. Even today, our emphasis on the family is misunderstood by the social services and the authorities. Why do we care so much about the family? Because it is a person's only refuge when all else fails; it is the only place where a person might still feel a welcome; it is the only place where one can still be "somebody." A person finds identity in the family. The children, the spouse, or the companion constitute a person's last refuge of freedom. Even if children are taken away, they remain a reference point for their parents. Because we emphasized the family, we were regarded as old-fashioned, which caused us great suffering but did not shake our resolve.

From the start, the decisive factor in the Movement was that we had only ourselves to offer. We owned nothing. We were not a housing organization or social workers sent by some ministerial department. We had only our hearts to offer. Living with the bare minimum and few resources made it possible for us to be accepted by the most disadvantaged families. We had no power whatsoever, political or social, nor did we have the support or the guarantee that comes from belonging to a religious denomination. We came empty-handed into the heart of poverty. We could only give what we were; that is, men and women determined to devote our lives to fighting alongside those who had been thrown into destitution. Our only objective was the people and their advancement and promotion. From the start, our aim was that those families who lived in utter poverty become the defenders of their own family members. We started from nothing, with no outside support or contacts, sharing with the families their condition of total destitution. The majority of them had known nothing but poverty, ignorance, illness, unemployment, and always rejection and exclusion. We wanted their own efforts to be the stepping stone back into society, as people responsible for themselves, their children, and their own lives. This practice aimed at bearing testimony to the worth of every human being, for no one is ever completely at the end of the road. If the poorest of the poor could to some extent live in an atmosphere of sociability and solidarity, even though trapped by poverty; if the disadvantaged were in a position to assert that life and society could have other mainsprings than consumerism and profit, it meant that a new world and a radical change of perspective could be offered to all people. We were proposing a different type of relationship and a different aim for our struggle.

Such a plan met with many difficulties. Our rich and prosperous society was unwilling or unable to see the reality of poverty, alleging that it had been done away with. Therefore we had to bear witness to what we heard, to what we saw, and to what we experienced. Proclaiming what we witnessed was not sufficient; the message had to be understood. This necessity led the Movement to set up its own Research Institute. We supplied the evidence for our claim; that is, not only do the very poor exist—they are here among us— but they bring to light the occasions when we do violence to our own convictions and contradict our own assertions and ideals by the life we impose on them. The setting up of the Research Institute was a political act in the full sense of the word; basing itself on evidence, the Institute denounced a situation, and it proposed measures. It also proved that people of all walks of life could join forces for a just cause; that is, to enable the disadvantaged to shoulder their own responsibilities. It demonstrated that to prevent these families from taking on their familial, social, political, and religious responsibilities was a violation of basic human rights.

Another point I want to stress is that, confronted with a rich society trying to ignore poverty, the Movement chose from the start to be interdenominational and interpolitical, rather than nondenominational or apolitical. I knew from experience how fortunate Catholics and believers in general are, in that their education has taught them to love others. I came across many institutions unable to work for the liberation of the destitute despite their desire to do so, and I felt we had to share the opportunity we have as believers. For me, everyone, no matter what their ideas, beliefs, or culture, has a legitimate right to descend to the lowest rung of the social ladder. It is hard to imagine how difficult this is for people who do not have the privilege of belonging to a church, as we do. Everyone should be able to turn the poorest families into a focal point, actively involved in the liberation of others. It is difficult to understand the suffering of persons who are confronted with destitution and who have not acquired at an early age a certain way of looking at others, of seeing the poorest as those with whom

Christ has totally and without reservation identified himself. In that respect, too, we do not always realize what we owe to the Church.

When confronted with destitution the first French volunteer, who was an atheist, relied on her sense of justice and her deep humanitarian feelings. She was profoundly affected, almost destroyed, by the failure of the poorest families. She cannot transcend or accept failure because for her there is nothing beyond failure. When I say that being interdenominational is an act of justice toward those who have not had the chance to be brought up with a special concern for others, there is no conceit in my words. Inside every person there is a seed of tenderness, which has to be brought to light and be nurtured from childhood on. The need to share with another person, to feel and take on the other person's suffering, and to turn this suffering into hope, can only be the fruit of education or conversion.

In our Movement, we see people as people first, not through the lens of a program or a structure. As long as we do not feel bound and confined by an organization, we can be free to live an ideal that is dependent upon the people themselves with whom we want to share it. In this way the poorest family can become the focal point, the center of concern for all. By making the most deprived person the center, we encompass all humankind through a single person. This does not mean limiting our vision but rather projecting it into the realm of love. Love has no confines; it cannot be imprisoned; it cannot be restrained. It is always folly.

We must unhesitatingly and boldly connect the poorest persons with Jesus Christ; they are one. We must unhesitatingly refuse to reject any human being, rich or poor, whether they are responsible for their situation or victimized by it. Love has no boundaries. All people are part of the same humanity and all share the same destiny.

When I finally arrived at the Noisy-le-Grand camp, I said to myself: Those destitute families will never be able to pull through on their own, but if I join them, they will climb the steps of the Elysée Palace, the Vatican, the United Nations, and all the great international organizations. They must become full members of our society. This idea, which was conceived on this barren land in mid-summer of 1956, might seem ridiculous to some people. Contemplating the world from Golgotha, Christ declared that he had conquered it. Anyone who makes the poorest person the focus of attention cannot fail to see the whole world, to see all of humankind in the same vision, leaving no one out. In a way, from this vantage point such persons can declare that they, too, have conquered the world.

And so, as if he were sharing a secret with us, almost confessing to us, Father Joseph reveals what is in his mind as well as what is close to his heart. To have been the recipient of such an "avowal" of his vision of humankind, of education, and of the Church, was a moving experience. The challenge was not to let it be just a passing emotion. How are we to live if we want this vision to become ours and to become a lasting one? This book aims at giving an answer. When he sent the completed manuscript to the publishers with the final corrections, Father Joseph appended this short note: "I pray that this book may fulfill its purpose, which is to make people love the Church and encourage many to join it in order to fight poverty." He makes us see and hear what has been seen, heard, and experienced by men and women within the Fourth World. Without the Fourth World Movement, society, in its forgetfulness, would be able to omit from its solidarity those whom its life and functioning had excluded. But then what kind of society, what kind of Church would this be? All the wonderful ideas about charity, brotherhood, justice, and generosity would be just a lie, the most damaging of all lies. Civilization would be perverted and the Church betrayed. This book affirms the refusal to let human solidarity be broken.

1

The Church Is the Church of the Poor

Gilles Anouil:[5] Publishing a book, especially a book like this one, is not an everyday or a neutral event. Father Joseph, why did you agree to write this book?

Father Joseph Wresinski: First of all, I thought it was important to be able to relate what families of the Fourth World have taught us over the last twenty-five years. These very disadvantaged families have taught me so much that I have no right to keep it to myself. It is my duty to transmit what I have learned to society, for its benefit, and to the Church, so that it becomes what it is called to be. Every worthwhile message has a right to be written down, and it should be a message for others, especially when it comes from the most disadvantaged. Once something has been written, it also enters history. If we manage to record the message of the Fourth World in writing, we will advance its cause.

Furthermore, I am a man of the Church and I devote my life to it. Therefore, my ideas and my thoughts are not my own. Similarly, my commitment to the most deprived people is not my own. It belongs to the Church—that, at least, is my deepest wish. What I have done in my life as a priest, I have undertaken in the hope of building the Church. I had to place stones one on top of another. It was more than introducing the most impoverished to the Church and it was more than making the Church a witness to their liberation. I had to place these families at the very basis of the Church, in its foundations.

That is one of the reasons I have always wanted to write a history of the poorest on a day-to-day basis. I have been doing this since the 1960s with those who surround me, in the certainty of discovering there the basic reality of the Church. I did, however, need time as I went on my way, to discover God's call and God's anguish expressing itself in the wretchedness and suffering of the Fourth World.

You say the Fourth World is the essential reality of the Church. Is the call to God stronger among these families than in the modern world in general?

I cannot say, but I can vouch for the interest shown by families in the slums every time they are asked to share their thoughts on the important questions they ask about life and death, about humanity and about God. Today I can bear witness to their need for God and for the Church.

The magnitude of this need struck me when I came to live among the inhabitants of the camp for homeless people in Noisy-le-Grand. The families often had neither chairs nor a stove. They lived in utter destitution. Yet when they talked about the Church, they talked as if they were talking about themselves: our Mass, our priest, our church.... They complained of not being visited by the priests, of not being at ease in their parish church, as if they had been robbed of their possessions. They protested as if they had been left outside the door of their own house. In a word, to hear them speak, you would have thought that the right to be the Church had been denied them. The Church was not an institution for them, nor was it part of their environment. They felt they belonged to the Church from the very depths of their being, and they said so straight out.

It took me some time to understand this. Nevertheless it was for the Church that I started writing about the daily life of the destitute so as to make their position in history known. My idea was that the Church could, in this way, find a concrete way of being recognized within a living people. At the time, I talked about it to Canon Boulard. After a moment's thought, he replied, "Don't delude yourself. Few people from the Church will read your books." I was disconcerted but not disheartened. The Church, it is true, is first and foremost a dwelling place, not something to be read about.

Didn't you find what Canon Boulard said to be a condemnation? Wasn't he saying that by losing interest in the poor, the Church was betraying the Gospel?

The Church does not lose interest in the poor. It cannot. Of course, it does turn away from them at times, but that is understandable. Destitution comes across as the opposite of grace. Those who do not know the people experiencing destitution see only rejected creatures to be treated with scorn, not people who are suffering; people at risk, ignorant and despairing, living in downtrodden families. They have become a threat to our very clean but weakened and sometimes cowardly consciences. How could we see them as our equals from the start? It would mean they could ask unlimited questions about ourselves and the society we are part of, about everything we experience and believe in. We would be admitting they carry the burden of our sins; seeing them as our equals would force us, in some way, to embrace the leper.

Clearly, Christianity should make heroism possible for everyone it touches. In the meantime, to be put in an awkward situation by those who are excluded is not easy to live with. We might turn away from them or accuse them. We no longer live in an age where proclaiming the beggar, the disfigured poor, or the leper a "child of God" has any meaning.

What time in history were you thinking of?

I was thinking of the Church in every age—because for the Church this time is not really over. The Church always proclaims that the poor are its flesh and blood, its deepest reality; it is not always evident that the Church lives this reality without wavering. But I am not distressed or outraged by this fact. The Church is the poorest. It is that by its very essence. And so, sooner or later, in a more or less concrete and lasting way, in a more or less hidden or public way, the poor are recognized by the Church and welcomed before anyone else.

Through its history the Church is condemned—if I may say so—to remember, to become aware again that it is poverty, an object of scorn and exclusion; that it is the unloved, the rejected of the world. It is forced to go to the most disparaged and excluded people. Pope Paul VI said: "The Church's mirror is Jesus Christ." That amounts to saying that the mirror of the Church is fallen humankind. The Church is not only in communion with the destitute. It is the destitute.

That is the Church in the plan of God. What is this plan? To save all human beings without exception. "Without exception," does not mean including the poorest but including the richest. In order to save all, Jesus Christ wanted to join them together in the most authentic part of their humanity: that which is not weighed down with riches, money, or honor. He had to be embodied in humanity, devoid of what is not truly human, stripped of all economic, political, and religious power. This is the humanity of the poorest, not of the wealthy. The essential core of humanity has not been damaged in the poor. Therefore Christ could be incarnated in them without difficulty.

However, you yourself have said that the poorest persons are damaged people.

It is true that the destitute are broken, undermined, and worn human beings. Destitution has prevented them from developing their intelligence and has at times reduced them to such a state of dependence that they are ashamed of being human. They are, however, human in an unadulterated stage, if I may say so. They suffer deeply from being despised. They know they are rejected and yet they refuse to be so. So, as soon as there is a glimmer of hope or the arrival of a prophet, they surround him, throng toward him, and crush him. Such was the case with Jesus Christ. The poor wanted to touch him so they could be freed. They rejected the way they were forced to live, and they wanted to hope. Jesus could not be incarnated in another group of society—whose humanity is cluttered, inoperative because of their possessions—however modest. Worldly goods overburden people, making them proud and vain. They can no longer strip themselves of their goods to become like the poorest and to welcome the most humble. In order to embrace and save humankind, Jesus was forced to be the least of the least, otherwise he would have been recognized by those who possess but not by the most humiliated people.

People will say you are preoccupied with the sordid aspects of life.

Jesus, the poorest of all, is anything but sordid. He adopted the condition of a slave, of utter destitution, in order to assert that humanity prevails, that people always remain free enough to free their brothers and sisters. Perhaps we do not stress enough that Jesus did not simply come to liberate humankind. He came and he surrounded himself with the poor, who would, together with him, free everyone. He wanted them to unite with him in wanting to free everyone, rich and poor.

In the meantime, we first have to acknowledge the Lord's choice to fully adopt the condition of the most despised—or shall I say, those belonging to the downtrodden classes. And he did this not only at the time of his birth and death but throughout his life. He lived the life of a man who was misunderstood and rejected and who showed that in the way he reacted to other persons and events. His words, his replies, his actions all point to a man who was constantly scorned. The gospels depict Jesus Christ as very much ill at ease in the world, suffering greatly, as do the underprivileged today. Like today's destitute families, his behavior drew the scorn of those around him. Christ was not pretending; he was poor.

For all that, the Church is not simply a "Cour des miracles"[6] (Court of Miracles) or a community closed in on itself. It is the very being of the Lord, who himself was poor and who wanted the poor to defend the rights he granted all human beings. He wanted them to love so deeply that they would sacrifice their lives for everyone. Jesus did not merely state that all human beings have rights because they are children of God. He wanted to create the contagion of love, thanks to the poor. For love eradicates anything that hinders, blocks, or stops what is essential. The Church is the Lord who, through love, makes himself poor, ridiculed, persecuted, and excluded. For him, human rights are founded on love, otherwise they are deception and indirect oppression. In order for the poor to remain authentic and to allow them to save their brothers and sisters, he kept on teaching and sharing love throughout his life on earth. He asked them to commit themselves to sacrificing their lives in the same way he sacrificed his so that no one would be lost. But only the poor could accept such a price from the outset. "My Father, I give you thanks for hiding these things from the wise and powerful and for revealing them to the humble."

In reality, you are introducing a dual concept. On the one hand, the families of the Fourth World, weighed down by poverty, must form the cornerstone of the Church. They personify its message. On the other hand, exclusion and rejection are the condition of the Church itself.

Yes. The Church will be mocked by the world and rejected. I discovered this as a young boy, raised by my mother, the poorest woman in the Saint-Jacques neighborhood of Angers. I learned to love the Church because my mother was a woman of prayer. Every morning she sent me to the Good Shepherd Convent. I was an altar boy there from the age of four and a half. I loved the beauty of the Church and the serenity of the nuns. Despite that, even as a child, I could sense the fragility of this community, remote from the neighborhood. I used to think, "The nuns have been driven away in the past; it can still happen now." Remember that, at that time, many people did not conceal their hostility toward the Church. One always saw the same people at

Mass; very few men attended. The principal of the public school went to another parish for fear that being seen in church would hinder his career. All that made me wonder. In the street, everywhere, posters ridiculed religious people. Sometimes, in a store, people would make jokes about churchgoers. There was a big discrepancy between the neighborhood and the church that happened to be in the middle of it. People would greet the parish priest in the street, but I did not feel it was quite sincere. I thought to myself, "The Church means nothing to any of these people."

As I grew up, I realized even more the lack of strength of the Church which was so criticized and put down. I saw priests and nuns made the target of ridicule, and on occasion, even verbally abused in the street. Around the time of Vatican II, I heard the Church being accused of pretentiousness and of possessing money and power, which I knew was not true. I myself have been affronted and insulted because of my cassock too many times to delude myself about the power of the Church. If Christians reflected on their memories, they would know that the Church, like Jesus and the poor, is at the mercy of all financial, political, and ideological powers.

As a child, didn't that bother you?

That did not bother me because the Church, for me, was the prayer of my mother. The Church was Mother's silences and her meditation. It was also the chaplain of the Good Shepherd Convent who, hundreds of times a day, would repeat, "My God, I love you, my God, I love you." The Church was the parish priest who, unlike our neighbors, showed respect to my mother. He used to come and ask her, poor as she was, for a donation for the clergy, and he would receive with great respect the coin that my mother gave him.

Looking back now, I see that, in my child's perspective, the personality of the Church was humble and vulnerable like my mother; its reality was the contempt that surrounded it. Perhaps it is for this reason that, when I see the world of the very poor today, I have no problem saying to myself: Here is the Church.

Against this Church, poor and servile, no one can do anything because its strength resides in its vulnerability. As long as it is like Christ—slandered, beaten, and spat upon—it will personify love, and the poorest will recognize themselves in it. The more it has fallen (and I insist on using this word) the more the destitute will know that it belongs to them, and the more ready they will be to find themselves in it, to join it in order to save the rich and those who are like themselves.

Isn't that the opposite of being preoccupied with the sordid aspects of life? Jesus did not leave the lame, the crippled, the blind, and the sick to their fate. He put an end to their distress. He gave speech to the dumb and hearing to the deaf. He also proposed to them a real project for society: to set ablaze a new fire on the earth so that those who have possessions abandon their heedlessness, their goods, their privileges, their defenses; that is, everything that prevents them from being fully human. Only then could they become devoted to the salvation of others.

When Jesus Christ says, and when the Church repeats after him, "Because of me and them, you will leave your fields and your house, your wife and children, you will sell all you have," it is not an allegory or a symbol. It means you will gain less profit and fewer privileges. So, the Church is an assembly of believers who know that liberation is in their hands. It is a community of people who have hope and who know that freedom is already gained: "The dumb speak and the lepers are healed." These were not bits of good advice or prophecies without immediate concrete implications. In the life of Christ himself, the paralyzed walked and the deaf heard. And the destitute were the first to recognize the Lord because Jesus thought and desired like they did, and he responded to their hope.

Didn't they abandon him at the crucifixion?

Did they abandon him? Or did they hide away, faced with the system and faced with those in power? In any case, from what I know, the poor are nostalgic for the Church. The poorer they are, the more they long for it. It is so slandered and there are so many lies told about it that they can't help but see themselves fully reflected in it. I have witnessed this. Each time they have a hint of presence of the Church, they feel comforted and reassured. Its presence in their midst makes them grow. The Church remains their basic community, where they do not even need to talk in order to be welcomed and understood. Thus, what a disappointment it is when the Church is unfaithful to them.

Furthermore, I think that in the Church, anything that does not express poverty—in theology, spirituality, apparel, or buildings—will sooner or later be swept away. But what will never disappear is my mother's prayer, when she was sitting motionless on her chair. What will never be swept away is the prayer of that man in the camp for the homeless in Noisy-le-Grand. It was two o'clock in the morning, I had restored peace in a family, and I was going back to my shack. Seeing a light in one of the Quonset huts, I knocked and went in. A man was sitting, his head in his hands. He laid his eyes on me without a word; then he said, "Well, I am glad you are here. I was just praying." His son-in-law had just died, drowned. I sat down next to him and we did not say anything more. We just prayed together that night, in that camp of the miserably poor. Nothing can destroy this prayer, and you will understand why I never worry about knowing whether the Church will accept the poor or not. It cannot reject them. It is they.

You have never, therefore, been outraged by the apparatus, the administration of the Church, not to mention its political role?

It is not I who say there are no grounds for revolt against the Church; it is God. The Church is not where we are looking for it, and God is not mistaken in this. The Church is not an apparatus or a power. It took me some time to understand this, even if I knew it intuitively as a child.

The Church is in the midst of the poor. This might be the reason why, wherever I lived, I was concerned with the state of the church as a building. Where there was none, I created a chapel, a place of prayer for proclaiming the Church's presence. In Noisy-le-Grand, the men of the camp and volunteers from four denominations built a chapel. When I watched men and women coming there on Christmas Day, on Good Friday, or for a funeral, I would sometimes think, "They come, but in fact they have nothing to gain, since they expect nothing from the Church." But I was wrong. They came because they knew they needed the Church. In their daily lives, they were nobody and counted for no one; or worse, they were always a burden or an embarrassment, a superfluous people, as if life would be better if they did not exist. But the Church, which proclaims throughout history the existence of God, which affirms the salvation of man in Jesus Christ who died and who was resurrected—this Church was, for these people, the only chance of being "someone." The Church alone, because it believed in them, was giving them the responsibility of saving their brothers and sisters.

It is commonly said that every person must be able to exist in the eyes of others. I believe that all people must be able to express their faith, knowing they will be taken seriously. The worst thing about great poverty is the inability to share what one believes. The Church, however, invites us to proclaim our beliefs. The families in Noisy-le-Grand knew that well; and that is why they used to come to church. The Church apparatus, the Church institution is not a real problem for the very poor. One of the most destitute mothers in the Noisy camp used to tell me, "You see, Father, I don't go to the chapel, but the fact that it is there—this reassures me."

Isn't it trying for you to feel that the Church is not more faithful to its message?

I always come back to the same point: I don't worry because I know the Church can't avoid for long seeing itself in the poor. It is already visible there in the person of many Christians, priests, and nuns. The day will come when it will assert this so strongly that the world will be transformed through it. This is a part of the Church's own prophecy, therefore there will come a day when it must re-assert that it is rejected by the world. On that day it will personify the refutation and rejection of the "sin of the world," which brings about the misery of extreme poverty.

Can you see any progress in this direction?

I don't know whether there is any need to talk about progress. There is a certain determinism, inevitability almost. I don't know how this can be avoided. The gospel keeps repeating its message over and over, with particular emphasis on the person of Jesus Christ. We have to come back to this fact incessantly. What do we see in the gospel other than a man buffeted by a society that rejects him? His divinity was expressed fully when he protested about the fate reserved for the poor, who are his people. He did not become defensive in the presence of the doctors of the law, the priests and politicians; nor was he their accomplice. His words, his actions, and the people he associates with not only confirm the dignity of the poor, but they also speak of the privileged place of the most excluded. His life and his miracles had the sole objective of asserting that these people were his priority. These poor, who did so much damage to his reputation in the eyes of the authorities, were the rejects of the temple. If we look at them closely, we find in these people who were despised the signs of misery, the world of the outcast.

I stress that we must watch them attentively. Those who pursue Jesus and who want to touch him, those who want to follow him, forgetting to take any food with them, they are not just "poor" people. Among these people we often recognize men, women, and children who have been shaped by extreme poverty. The Lord surrounds himself with those who are mistrusted or disapproved of by Pharisees and doctors. The authorities did not discard or despise the courageous people who lived a poverty-stricken life at the time; but they defended themselves against all those who appeared to be asocial, marginal, and maladjusted, those who did not fit in with the structures of a poor rural society. However, it was often in those people that Jesus Christ recognized himself.

Having said this, if there is infidelity on the part of the Church, even in this betrayal lies a chance for humanity. For when the Church is not in tune with the world of the very poor, somehow the Church is aware of that. This fact forces the Church to confront its own disappointment, its failure at times; it is led to face reality. If the Church recognizes it has failed—and who would dare say they have never failed—it is then forced to mend its ways and renew itself; but it also serves as a mirror of the world's failure. When the Church is ill at ease, it becomes a reminder of the questions the most deprived people pose to the world. In any case, has this ever been otherwise? I do not think the poorest, even in the Middle Ages, have ever been in complete agreement with the Church or with society. This failure is, however, in itself a message to the world. If the Church fails, a Church that is and knows it is the Church of the poor, what then about the world? What about our societies which do not really know what to do with the poor? In its failure the Church reminds society of its own failure.

Is there not a parallel to be drawn with Marxism? Marxism also has a message of liberation and it also fails in its daily reality. Is that not the fundamental questioning with which it is confronted: that once it is put into practice, it becomes altered? Would Marxism then be defined as a protest and a chance for the world, just like the Church?

I am not sure about the analogy. Some Marxists are men and women who are out of the ordinary. They believe in what they say and are willing to sacrifice their lives for it. There are, however, fundamental differences between Marxism and the Church. First of all, the Marxist message is not directed to the very poor. At least I have not found anything resembling the Good News announced to the poorest. But it is true that Marxism is often talked about very lightly. Its history is also interpreted as being unfaithful to the human person, as a failure in itself rather than as a reminder to the world of its failure. If Marxism does fail, it is a common failure, at least toward the poor; the whole Western world has failed in regard to extreme poverty. Capitalism has not brought about the liberation of the most disparaged and most oppressed people. It is sometimes said that the West excluded from its bosom those who did not relate to its values. But in fact the reality is more serious and more profound; that is, the Western world excluded those who did not buy into its weaknesses, to its obsessive yearning for happiness, material gain and personal success. In this respect, the failure of Marxism is also a message to everyone, a message to the Western world. We failed together. In the same way, should there be a failure of the Church, the failure is mine, ours. We have all avoided doing enough. But in a deeper sense, the difference between Marxism and the Church is Jesus Christ himself who, having emptied himself, asks us to get rid of our trappings in order to meet the very poor and to be taught by them.

Marxists believe that there are saving systems or structures. They do not believe that the poorest and most miserable would ever decide to work for change. Neither do they believe that affluent people could leave everything for the sake of the underprivileged. Do Marxists follow through on their faith in the human person? The question is for them to answer. The Christian belief is that slaves cannot live without freedom. To gain freedom, they constantly invent new ways. They love freedom; they aspire to it as a vital need. Beyond desiring freedom for themselves, they can aspire to it for everyone. Total freedom—that of being free before God, free to love, to share, to obey, and to refuse. This is the way Christians recognize love, and they believe it can be contagious for all. For them, it is structures and systems that enslave, that can never be long-term liberators.

Should we think that humanity can never achieve its ideal?

Perhaps it would be better to say that humanity never stops pursuing the prophecy God promised to fulfill. When people commit themselves to a grand ideal, they really believe they will succeed. The Communists I know believe firmly that, through them, people will free themselves from oppression and exploitation. They therefore embody a fragment of hope in the world. In this way, they are living a prophecy: this will happen, this will be, and this is.

The difficulty with Marxism is that there is nothing beyond the present life. It is condemned to having to succeed now, immediately. The Church's situation is quite different. It has already succeeded, and its success cannot be disputed. Despite all the Church's failings, the poor are already liberated. Their liberation is accomplished not only in Jesus Christ but also in all believers. Believers, whoever they are, whether they profess their faith, whether they are in a state of prayer, or whether they are protesting against injustice, are liberators by this very fact. Why? Because they become part of the faith, the prayer and the protest of the poor. They are poverty and destitution. Not everyone is aware of the chance thus given to them. However, the very existence of believers in the midst of the world is the reality of and witness to extreme poverty embodied and revealed before human beings.

Pope John XXIII's announcement at the beginning of Vatican Council II: "The Church is the Church of the poor," was a reminder of the proclamation "The Good News is proclaimed to the poor." This seems to me to be the essential message of Vatican II, the proclamation that is self-sufficient and sums up the whole council. Not that I think it has been fulfilled on this earth. But this prophecy is already fulfilled in God and is the only one the Church has to fulfill if it wants to save all human beings. This prophecy has to be constantly recalled: we are the poor and the rejected, we are the wretched and excluded. Not to recognize this reality involves more than being unfaithful; it means being an accomplice in sin.

When you say that believers are poor, in what sense do you understand this? Are they poor in the sense that they will never settle on this earth; that they will always live as nomads in tents; that they will only be passing through? Are believers poor only because they know that nothing material or spiritual belongs to them?

Of course this, and more. To be a believer is to be on a passionate quest for the one who is a witness to the reality of the Lord here on earth. Because the gospel commands us not only to "leave everything you have," but "go toward." Not only "Leave your family," but "Go toward those who already accomplish, through their existence, what you must become: someone despised, someone laid bare, someone unfaithful to the world, who is consequently someone excluded."

The Lord does not say, "Go toward those who are despised by others," but "Go toward those who have no one to despise them, who are totally abandoned, ignored by you and by everyone. Go toward the lost sheep of the flock, toward the one who will be your burden, because, having remained alone for a long time, they might not even understand their condition and consequently what you want of them. Go and reveal to them that they are the Lord calling, that they are the reality of the Church itself."

It is perhaps wrongly said of Marxism that it tends toward equality at the base, that it brings everyone to a lower level. We forget that Christ commands us to love from the bottom up, and to Christ that is not a low level. Love for the poorest is the most difficult. Perhaps worldly equality and justice from the bottom up are degrading. I do not believe this. In any case, there is no other salvation for Christians, who are people of faith and of meditation, than to find in their hearts and in their lives those who are the lowest in the world. And it is not sufficient to give away one's possessions, to recognize oneself in the poor, and to consider them as equal; they have to become one's privileged daily partners. That is why it is so difficult for Christians to accept the Church of the poor. It is really alien to the world. How can the world admit this? The very existence of the Church thus becomes a dangerous protest to the world. Those who embrace this lose all other points of reference. How can they not look back, not be afraid when they see their prestige and security being abandoned? The world is afraid and does everything it can to prevent the Church from bearing that message.

Doesn't the Church itself hinder the expression of this message of Jesus Christ?

No. It is the world that feels troubled and does not want to listen. The world does not worry much about the Christian ethic, and it can always argue about dogma. But it cannot deny the reality that in the Church and in its message the poorest are equal to all. I mentioned earlier the "lepers" in our society whom you have to embrace as if they were the only ones who mattered to you—not only as brothers and sisters but also as companions for life. The Church carries this within itself. It proclaims it, whether it wants to or not.

You said, however, that destitution was the opposite of grace. Now, according to you, it is, on the contrary, grace itself?

I said that destitution was the opposite of grace because it is a product of sin. Someone who falls into the water becomes a drowned person and a drowned person is the opposite of someone alive on the bank. This image of someone about to drown frightens and repulses us; nevertheless, a person drowning has to be saved, and Jesus says this person has to be saved first. Jesus asserts that our salvation depends on this: that person is a measure of our commitment to God and to God's plan on earth. In reality, this person, so weakened by destitution to the point of being unrecognizable in our eyes, in the eyes of the world, is someone underdeveloped materially, socially, and spiritually. Poverty is like absolute underdevelopment. However, its victims are the first ones saved by the Lord; as for the Church, it is through these victims that grace passes.

To use an image: The poorest are the artery through which blood must flow to sustain the whole body. If the artery is blocked, the whole body dies. For the Church, the poor are the artery, and to clear that artery is a matter of life or death. If grace passes through the poorest, the whole body is nourished.

I was talking to you about a very poor man whom I had found praying in a Quonset hut in the camp for the homeless. When I found him there in the middle of the night and sat down next to him as he let grace flow through him, I was the Church receiving the grace of God for all. Christ tells us that without this man, without the poorest, there is no Church. The Church does not exist if the Fourth World is not within it. Without the Fourth World, no religious celebration is possible. Without the Fourth World, which lets grace stream in, the table is bare and will stay that way.

The gospel affirms this, and the personal presence of Christ among us bears witness to nothing else. We remember well his command to go and evangelize and baptize. But we forget the heart of the Lord's message: Go and baptize those who live in the back alleys, those who have not been invited to the meal because of their wretched situation and humiliating life. Go and see the long-term unemployed, those whose fathers already had no recognized or respected employment; go and see children who do not benefit much from school, mothers who are penniless, families who are housed in dilapidated slum areas of ill-repute. We willingly forget to gather those people. However, it was for them that the command to go and baptize was given.

Jesus Christ defined himself by his birth and his death, and without doubt all human beings define themselves in this manner. Christ's message and his life are defined in the same way. The first witnesses to the love of God at the Lord's birth were the shepherds. They were despised, excluded people who led a primitive existence not approved of by the rural, sedentary population of Israel. These shepherds did not attend religious rites or feasts because, in the organization of religious life, their situation had not been taken into account. They could not attend rites at a given time. They were so despised that they were not accepted as witnesses before the law. Their word was not trusted because they were seen as cursing God—the reverse of grace as seen by the people of Israel. But it was precisely through them that Jesus Christ made grace flow.

There were also the three wise men…

The three wise men were in search of truth. We shall certainly come back to this point. But first there were the shepherds, who were not searching and who received without asking. They were present at the very start of the Good News, at a time when Christ was not yet speaking. Christ began to proclaim his message by gathering the most excluded persons around him, those who were "marginalized," as we say nowadays. I have already made the point that such people were found near Jesus throughout his life, and he himself lived the unsettled and hounded life of someone excluded. He also would be left out, and would die disparaged, shouted down, and humiliated like all those who are scorned by society. That is what Golgotha is: the act that sums up everything, Christ with marginal people, outside the city and among those who are officially kept out. For him, it was not a matter of acting as a poor or lower class person. It was a matter of being poor and of making the poor the privileged witnesses of God in the world. We could say today that they were the first defenders of human rights. Christ was the cornerstone, and he made the poor the spiritual life of the Church for centuries to come.

That is why the Church is repeatedly forced to reintroduce rejected people—those of the Fourth World—into its midst. If it does not reintroduce them into the building, it will collapse. Of course, according to Christ, that is not possible. It does matter if the Church is unfaithful through some of its members. However, none of this disturbs me. In all the struggles I have had, at first in the workers' world when I was a pastry cook, then in a factory, and finally in the Fourth World, I always felt perfectly at ease in the Church. It encouraged me and it represented grace.

Don't you see the Church rather as it should be or as it will be one day?

No, I see it as it is, in depth, as it is compelled to be. It cannot help being the song of the poor and their prayer, their society and their liberation. I told you I felt this when I was a child: in one way or another, in some part of the world or in some part of its people, the Church is being stripped and condemned to silence. The full reality of the prophecy always exists somewhere in the world. It exists in priests who are forbidden to celebrate Mass, but also in those Christians who are rejected, not because of some human struggle, but because they proclaim the reality of the Church as poor and fallen.

These people really are rejected. One example impressed me deeply: the little Brothers of Charles de Foucauld were forbidden to go barefoot in the port of Cairo. This was fifteen years ago, I think, when they were trying to work among a people who went barefoot, who were laborers in the port. The government did not stop them from working with the laborers, but it refused them permission to go barefoot, that is, to bear the external signs of a Church that was identifying with the poor in the most literal sense. They refused to allow the Church this image of itself.

Coming back to this other image—of the artery that must not be blocked—were you thinking of the mystical body and of the communion of saints?

Whenever a poor person anywhere in the world is excluded, it is the whole Church that is excluded. When, somewhere, a family hiding in a hovel or a slum is threatened with eviction, the whole Church suffers and fights against the eviction. The Church is in a state of sin if it does not protest. I do not say the Church must be everywhere, always bringing the bread that is needed, providing money, a roof, or work. Its fundamental vocation is to give God. But if it does not recognize itself in the starving, the wandering, the pauper, and the uneducated, then it is not the Church, and there is no Church-reality in the world. Because then grace is not circulating freely enough and cannot be life-giving, keeping both the Church and humanity alive.

The man whom I spoke about, praying in his utter misery, was the link, the channel bringing the whole of the Church back to God. From the very fact of their state of abandonment and shame, the poorest people form an essential part of the mystical body. They have a unique and essential message because of their very situation and the suffering it inflicts. We cannot carry out a valid reflection in the Church without taking into account what the poorest tell us about being humiliated, about Christ being crucified. That their words are scarcely audible does not change anything; that they are merely a cry or a plea for help does not change anything. I would even go so far as to say that the less elaborate the cry, the more unpolished the word, the more it represents truth and richness for all. The more elementary the message, the more it is filled with experience and life and the more vital it is to the Church. The Church cannot formulate its theology, its spirituality, or its liturgy without that message.

Don't we run the risk of becoming content that the poor exist, otherwise what would become of us?

It is not a question of our being satisfied with the condition of the poor, but of transforming it by taking the poor as our partners and our guides. Jesus Christ identified with the poorest of his time, and he still does and always will identify with the poorest at all times. Their lives, therefore, are also his own and so are the source of our spirituality. Is it possible for us to work out a theology of the human person without starting from the most impoverished? How can we develop a liturgy without the prayer and the cry of the poor? If the Church did not benefit from the wealth offered by the world of the excluded, it would be amputated, incomplete, and unfinished in its expression; furthermore, it would not be the mystical body.

But, Father Joseph, this analysis you make along the lines of the Gospel is not just applicable to the Church. You could say the same thing about society and the different forms of humanism.

I do not think so. Humanism views humanity through individuals. The fundamental difference is that the Church does not look at human beings as an ultimate end. It looks at them as a mirror, reflecting its own image back to it. The Church itself is in question, not a certain idea about human beings or a feeling of solidarity with them.

Doesn't that apply also to humanism, at least insofar as it is an expression of solidarity with human beings?

That is precisely what the Church is not, an expression of solidarity. The Church is the suffering of people. Wherever there is poverty and suffering, excuse me for repeating this, it is the Church that suffers because Jesus Christ suffers. People and humanism can only bring help to other people. They will bring material or educational aid to the families of the Fourth World, or a job, or housing. They will provide the means available to a society. They defend human rights, and this is necessary; some would reproach them if they did not provide these gestures of solidarity. As for the Church, it is quite different. It loves, it brings salvation and the revelation that "the other" is saved in the same way I am and, I would say, even before me.

The Church is not only a service rendered or a right allocated; it is a reality experienced through brothers and sisters who are traveling companions. We must not reproach the Church for not limiting itself to the defense of human rights. Its role goes much further than this. The issue, as regards the Church, is to know whether it finds its identity in the poorest and whether they find their salvation through it. What counts is not first what the Church brings but what it considers itself to be. And in the Church, the issue is not first our role as citizens, but our very being or reality as sons and daughters of God.

Saint Peter reminds us that we are all priests and children of God. Whatever interpretation we give to this, the fact remains that we are all of the same blood and we have all been given the same mission. The Lord asks us to acknowledge this fact, which implies more than just recognizing the rights of our neighbor. This is all the more difficult if we take things literally. Vatican II did so, and it was that Council which entered fully into the prophetic history of the Church by asserting it is the Church of the poor.

This prophecy was nevertheless not very new.

I'm afraid I must contradict you. This proclamation was new in that Pope John XXIII made it into something of a prerequisite, a condition, that is, the touchstone of the reliability of the Church. He proclaimed that the measure of the success of the Council—as of the Church of tomorrow—was awareness of this reality. This prophecy was so new that some people were somewhat perturbed, perhaps because the Church fathers did not always try to learn about the place of the most rejected persons in the Church. With this proclamation, we were offered the means of taking up their suffering, their prayer, and their protest. Did we seize the opportunity?

The basic problem was to know whether the post-conciliar Church would engage in prayer, reflection, and meditation on its own reality as the community of the poorest. The question was not whether it would stand in solidarity with the poorest, but whether it would be the authentic place for the prayer, the song, and the demands of the poor. Would the Church, through its worship and liturgy, represent the hope of the poor ascending toward God?

The community of the poor is not a community apart from the Church, and it is not required to be anything other than itself. If the Church is totally aware of what it is, the Church's prayer will be the prayer of the fallen and of families burdened by extreme poverty.

Since I have known you, I have often asked myself whether you were a priest because of Jesus Christ or because of your love for the poorest.

The question shouldn't have to be asked. In my youth, there was a time when I stood aloof from the Church. I was learning a trade, training to be a pastry cook, just entering the real world. At eighteen, when I joined the Young

Christian Worker movement, I started to pray again and to think of freeing my brothers. It was then that I thought of becoming a priest. To pray in the Church—to offer the Eucharist—meant to bring the gospel to my brothers and sisters, that is, to all those who led a life similar to my mother's. To struggle for them so that no family would ever be like my own meant becoming a priest of Jesus Christ, who died and rose from the dead. You cannot imagine how wonderful this time was. I knew then that my life was part of an eternal plan, that the poor would be evangelized, and that I would be contributing to a change of heart for other people. For me, everything was linked together. To have found faith again meant not only discovering the meaning of the struggle—which I already had—but also devoting my life to Jesus Christ.

So it was not through solidarity with the poor?

Absolutely not. One cannot avoid asking oneself the question: Are you a priest out of love for Jesus Christ or to engage in a social or political struggle? To reply, I would say that my whole experience as a child taught me about the connection between the Church and the poor, and their common destiny in Jesus Christ.

I knew this community through my mother. When we had nothing to eat, she would sit down and pray. I knew it through the Good Shepherd nuns who offered us soup every day, and through the priests from my childhood, who surrounded my mother with esteem and affection. My experiences elsewhere showed me that people are far more prone to despise, neglect, and ridicule the poor than to include them in their lives. The Church was different. It did not ridicule them. And also, the parish priest, the chaplain, and the nuns themselves seemed to be defenseless and poor as poor can be. I always had the feeling that there was a partnership. I thought that by becoming a priest, I was going home among my people. I also thought I was meeting up with Jesus who alone could give an essential and global response to the world of extreme poverty. Jesus Christ is the response awaited by the most disadvantaged persons.

Perhaps I should add, at the risk of surprising you, that throughout my childhood and into my adult life, I never met anyone in the Church who was not sensitive to the distress of other people. Not out of pity or in order to have a clear conscience, but because people recognize they are related to the suffering of others. Due to a relationship that has its source in original sin, are not Christians aware that they too are poor human beings, weak and cowardly before God, other persons, and even themselves?

Then, the weakness of the Fourth World would be a sort of parable of our own weakness?

Exactly. The Fourth World is at once our mirror and a sign of our hope. The poorest know this, too, and they represent our chance. They understand what we are, and they stop us from doing many a stupid thing and from being evil to the end. No, the poorest are not easily fooled. I have always been amazed at their talent for judging us, not because of what we seem to be or say or do, but because of what they see as weak, petty, or untrue. At the same time, however, they have a kind of sixth sense that recognizes our capacity for love.

In short, it was through my struggle among the poorest, and by giving priority to their way of seeing things, that one day I awakened to the reality of the Church; so much so that I believed I had to become a priest. No one becomes a priest without a deep-rooted attachment to Jesus Christ—an attachment to him not as a symbol but as a living reality, reflecting what the world experiences and what the poorest around us express and hope. The priest is compelled, one way or another, to want to model his life on the life of Jesus Christ. Otherwise he does not remain a priest. The life of the Lord in the world is that of a child born in a place where only children of marginalized people, such as shepherds, could be born. He belonged to a family without money or lodging, expelled from society; he lived among persons without work, ridiculed even in suffering, and whose pain was considered to be their own fault. For Jesus, the fault that led him to Golgotha was that he loved too much.

2.

The Life of the Poorest Is a Source of Grace

Gilles Anouil: You mentioned grace, which either flows or doesn't. But what is grace?

Father Joseph Wresinski: Grace is God getting hold of you and making you love others to the point of wanting them to be greater than you, better, more intelligent than you. Grace is the love that sees others as equal and wants them to be happier than oneself; that wants others at any price to love fully, with all their heart. It is God who goads us into wanting others to be able to free the world from poverty, and therefore from injustice, war, and hatred. God leads us where we do not want to go. Grace is "more," knowing that we are not just a distant reflection of God, but that the Lord is permanently present and living in us.

For us, grace means we should identify ourselves fully with the poorest because we have the same origin and belong to the same priestly race. It also means wanting to share the full measure of what we have received and to enable them to receive it in their turn. I am referring to the full measure of grace given by God. This should result in their also wanting that full measure of grace for us: this "more" already living in them.

As you see, I am repeating what the Church says about grace, and I am adopting it in my own way. This approach has been very useful to me in my life. I am a man of action, an impatient man. The will to find in other persons not only a brother or sister but also an equal or someone greater than myself, has prevented me from taking extreme positions and from going too far. This stopped me, for instance, from becoming a follower of Marxism. In my eyes, only the Church can give true equality, in birth and death. And after more than fifty years of that awareness, I still see only the Church endowing this equality without preconditions, not as a right to be granted or gained but as a state into which we are born. That is why I am affected by certain steps being taken nowadays concerning the sacraments.

Do you mean to say that priests set the conditions?

They ask for guarantees in order to administer sacraments, which are in themselves sources of grace. Can you imagine asking the poor for guarantees before allowing them to celebrate the sacraments of baptism and first communion, the sacrament of the sick; to celebrate their wedding and have it blessed by God? If you wish to have your children baptized nowadays, you are asked to show your credentials. If you ask that your children celebrate their first communion, some priests may not just take your present wishes into account but also ask for assurances for the future. It is as if the Son of God, whose death and resurrection are the only true guarantees, was requesting a birth certificate and papers showing that you are bona fide.

You do not accept this requirement, that believers make some kind of commitment. Does it shock you to see the Church asking for a commitment that children will persevere?

I understand the request for a commitment, but isn't the life of the poorest itself the greatest guarantee of commitment? It is a fact that they are destined to live the life of the Lord. Anyhow, asking them for guarantees indicates our belief that we speak the same language as they do. But this is not so. We do not know their language. To make up for this, we should be able to understand, without words, exactly what they ask of us. We need real sensitivity and a solid comprehension of the world of poverty to grasp what a mother means when she asks that her child be baptized, and what a father means when he lets his wife take the initiative and follows her lead. We do not know really what the guarantees of their perseverance will be. In whose name would we deny their right to grace? We are incapable of understanding their request, and we do not have the necessary information to judge it. How can we judge what people will do in the future? And even if we could, is it up to us to judge?

To deprive the poor of the sacraments—and consequently, of participation in God's life—seems to me an injustice. God gives the sacraments freely so that we can receive what is needed to love and to derive strength from love, to base our life on love. Why should we deprive the poorest and those who are the most thirsty for love? God is not a possession of the Church, not a God to be manipulated. The Church merely hands on what it receives from Jesus Christ, who is forever the poor one of the Father, attracting everyone to him. It is up to him to separate the wheat from the chaff when he finds that the time is right.

These requests for guarantees are more appropriate, perhaps, when made to the middle class?

I do not know if they are appropriate for anyone. They might seem adapted to the life of the rich: taking part in meetings and exchanges, and getting together with couples of the same culture who are believers. All this seems feasible when one is more or less well housed, respected for one's professional qualifications, and assured of a reasonable integration into the job market. This has nothing to do with the poorest; they do not even understand what we ask of them.

For my part, I observe that the poorest in our cities and towns are neither evangelized nor baptized. Their children are no longer taken into account. This situation is different from what I saw in the fifties and sixties in the poorest neighborhoods. And it is much more serious than it appears because this type of caution—I would say suspicion—on the part of the priests is taken by the poor as rejection, a rejection not only of their requests but of their very selves. Such a rejection is the last straw—the Church rejecting itself.

If there is an appropriate question to be posed, it should not be about a commitment made by the parents who come to ask for baptism or communion for their children. Rather, it should be a question of the Church's commitment to them. We ask the parents for a guarantee; whereas we, who have the chance of welcoming a poor family and of talking to them of God, should guarantee that we will never abandon them again. To welcome someone poorer than ourselves is always a privilege and a responsibility.

The Church should therefore commit itself to perseverance?

Obviously. You would not ask a cripple to walk; you would ask those around to help the person walk. And you would do so with such respect that the disabled person will feel like a whole person. The commitment is up to the Church, which wishes to become the instrument, I would say, of God's goodwill. Only God gives guarantees through grace. Even the most fervent parents cannot guarantee that their children will continue to love other people. We cannot predict anything; and, especially in matters involving God, we cannot pretend we are Madame Soleil [7] and know the future.

However much you respect the Church, do you set yourself above these kinds of regulations?

No, it is not a question of asserting my independence. In truth, I haven't the courage to apply the rule. I have never had the courage, even when I was a parish priest, to refuse my equals anything they have a right to through birth. There are things that cannot be refused on any account. But if I agree to answer a request (for the sacraments), I am committing myself. Agreeing to the request commits me to reconsidering things, to meditate and change, so that what the Church has given will not be lost. The question is whether I was converted through my contact with those persons. Did I recognize myself in them, and did I understand Jesus Christ better through this meeting? Did I make the necessary commitment to become poorer myself and to pray? These people were closer to Christ than I. They knew more about the Lord because they were living everything that Jesus had lived. Did I take this opportunity to know and love them better? Did I let them reveal Jesus Christ to me?

I am thinking of a man who was living with a woman in a common law marriage. They had seven children, and after some time both parents wanted them all to be baptized. They went to meet the parish priest, a remarkable man. But he presented them with a string of requirements: the family had to take part in such and such a meeting; the older children had to join a specific youth group. They all went one time. Then the father came to see me. He was disheartened because, at the meeting there had not only been talk of God but also of political and trade union commitment. "You know," he said, "I can't go any more; anyhow, I feel like an idiot. They talk and I don't understand what they are talking about." Then this father added, "What I hear there is what I overhear in the cafe every day."

If parents of catechumens find at those meetings the same talk that goes on in business or political meetings, what do they learn that is truly new and revolutionary? Where is the promised renewal that is to completely change their lives? That man never set foot in a single parish meeting again. And in the end, I obtained special permission to celebrate his marriage to the mother of his seven children and to baptize them all.

Despite your love for the Church, you have just questioned its rules. You ask about the Church's commitment to the perseverance of the destitute. Do you think that because the Church is more and more engaged in temporal affairs, it talks too much about people and society and too little about God?

I think the Church is somewhat elitist in its attitude, first of all by assuming it has the right to judge the capacity for love, prayer, and commitment of a people whose language and sensitivity it does not know. It would not act the same way with Muslims because it would respect their way of praying and their specific sensitivity. The Church does not always show such respect, however, to its own poverty-stricken people in the West who are of no denomination but who want to believe and love. Yet, such people are an "unfamiliar soil" and, furthermore, a soil awaiting the seeds that can germinate and grow. If the Church does not understand these people, by what right can it impose a commitment that is, moreover, of a temporal rather than a religious nature?

I do not condemn the Church, if that is what you ask. Like any other person, priests, too, can express their opinions concerning trade unions or politics. But how do we know if trade unions or political commitment are the true reflection of a love devoted to the Lord? Everything depends on a person's training and living conditions. It also depends on the interests we defend in political or trade union action. If we take up the fight for the poor, whether they are unionized or not, then yes, we love as Christ loved when he died on the cross. Otherwise, our intention is not clear; and in any case, temporal commitments are not of the same order.

According to the words of the gospel, which are often quoted out of context, you are saying that there are several dwelling places in the house of the Father.

When people live in emergency housing, in the infernal noise of the neighborhood and the constant quarreling, and still keep their share of tolerance toward one another, don't you think they are showing love and commitment to one another? When people are condemned to living constantly in overcrowded conditions, and they remain welcoming, do they not show solidarity and a real love for others? I know people who have practically nothing to eat at home and who would not leave a neighbor without some soup or bread. As long as they have some left at home, then the neighbors will have their share. I am thinking of a family who welcomed a neighbor's child on a permanent basis. This family had not enough to eat themselves and yet they would not let the young boy next door go to bed hungry. That family, living in filth and constant strife, was certainly receiving grace.

I firmly believe that the life of the destitute is a source of grace. They must be given anything that could serve to increase their grace. We should never cease to note the help and the acts of tenderness they offer each other despite all the hardships they undergo. We should never cease to discover the humble gestures that generate grace, the humble prayers they repeat endlessly in silence. They have already given their guarantees by overcoming their disappointments and their mistrust toward us, which are so legitimate. Even in their misery, they take a decisive step; they dare say to us, "I do love and believe... despite all the contempt that weighs on me, I come to assert my dignity as a child of God." What an opportunity for a priest or for a parish! Instead of turning up our noses or being fussy, we should have grand celebrations for their baptisms, first communions, and weddings. They were lost along the way, and they found their way again. Above all, they have so much to teach us about extreme poverty and our responsibility to eliminate it.

The Church seems to have neglected trade union and political realities for a long time. It is still reproached for not going far enough in these matters. Perhaps because of a guilty conscience, does it let the pendulum swing too far in the opposite direction?

I do not know if the Church has been as neglectful as is said and, in any case, I will not criticize it. It has had to recast itself in the mold of each period of time. It has had to adopt what society offered to transmit its message. This requires the Church's time and effort again and again. But I do not wish to talk about this. Beyond the need to adapt to changing realities, there remains this essential, unchanging responsibility: to seek out the poorest and welcome them in the Church's bosom. It neither offers them a blank check nor makes demands on them. The Church must look for them and carry them within itself. It must listen to them and let itself be transformed by them. Why should it listen to the world in preference to the poor, to whom the Lord has given the mission of teaching and educating the Church?

Should that stop the Church from preaching about trade unions and politics?

Not at all. But the Church must certainly not talk about these as others do. Christians have to go the limit in reaching out to all of humanity. They can never be satisfied until they reach all people, the poorest as well as the richest. They cannot raise an issue without seeing its human aspect, without asking how it affects the poorest. Christians cannot think in terms of politics or business without reference to this hidden part of the Church—its most distressed part, its hidden depths, which the world does not see. We must always respond to the appeals for more justice, at the same time asking: Justice for whom? For us, the real question is always: "More justice, but for whom?"

A nun has just become a member of the Fourth World volunteer corps, which is entirely devoted to the excluded people on all continents. Her religious order agreed to her wish to become a member, but with reservations. As a nurse, she was a committed trade unionist and she belonged to the workers' union at her hospital. When she told her fellow union members she was joining the Fourth World, they said to her, "You're going to waste your life. You are betraying our struggle by joining the world of inefficient people."

Whether they like it or not, the fate of Christians as trade unionists and politicians is to end up with inefficient people, not so much as their spokespersons but as people who identify with them. This nun came to us because, in the large hospital where she was committed to union matters, she was longing to identify with the destitute and to worship Jesus Christ through them. She realized that her companions in the union were generally involved with men and women who were already standing on their own two feet and who already knew how to voice their concerns. Union demands were always for certain categories of persons, excluding cleaning women and orderlies. All those around her, in her community and the trade union, were in contact with the visible part of the world—the part you feel comfortable with, whose problems you understand because they are well defined and defensible. The parents I spoke of earlier, who wanted to have their seven children baptized, would have been embarrassed to meet those nuns and trade unionists. The struggle union people carry on would have no relevance for that family. The family needed contact with people such as the nun who just joined our team, who would make the utmost effort to involve the family, and in the process receive grace through them.

Does that not presuppose we know how to identify the inefficient people or the invisible part of humanity? While I'm not completely ignorant, I myself did not know this. It might be that I refused to know. Christians, however, often lack this knowledge. I imagine that 99 percent of the population do not know there are two million disadvantaged people in France. For them, poverty is a symbolic and quite vague term. They might think of a beggar they meet after Mass or perhaps of unemployed people in a depressed region.

As the world does not want to see the Church as a servant and poor, it also does not want the destitute and the families most devastated by poverty, to be visible. The world finds ways not to call them poor. The world forces them into a masquerade, a clown act, showering them with false names, making them appear maladjusted or irredeemable. It describes them with adjectives that imply they are responsible for their situation. This is exactly how Jesus Christ was regarded—as being at fault rather than as a victim.

This is normal behavior for the world. Human beings have a need to see humanity as beautiful and to see the poor in their best light. However, such behavior is not at all normal for Christians who are committed to a political or a social struggle. Christians have to follow their own logic to the very end. They find themselves facing Christ at any given moment, not the resurrected Christ but the crucified Christ who was reproached and rejected; Christ who was constantly doubted because of his message but also because of his lifestyle and the people with whom he lived.

This is the source of my deep trust in the Church. All through its history, it has periodically found itself in a dilemma. It was obliged to recognize the face of Christ in the life and flesh of the destitute; and it found this impossible to do without blatantly contradicting the society of its time. We shall, no doubt, have to speak again about these periods of open persecution that recur regularly, because the Church cannot ignore for long those persons rejected by the world. To constantly have to awaken love for those who are excluded prevents Christians from assuming the nastiness that is often rife in the world of politics. As Michel Rocard said to me one day, "When faced with the aggressiveness characteristic of the political scene, sooner or later Christians lose their bearing." Love causes them to lose their way in politics, and that is to the glory of the Church, even if that earns the Church more contempt than respect.

It is true that Christians do not seem to be able to live in conflict for long?

At any given time, love loses its way in politics when it is faced with the kind of justice everyone talks about. Sooner or later, Christians can no longer be satisfied with justice alone. Whether they like it or not, they are forced to come to terms with the concept of justice itself, when it consists of setting salary scales, allowances, pensions, and prestige according to the person's qualifications. Christians see this type of justice as insignificant to Christians because they cannot help wanting more for persons whose role is seen as unimportant. They are forced to demand the best for the least educated child. In a sense, they have to violate the law of equality for the benefit of the person who has nothing and who is not even recognized as having any rights. Christians have to bend the rules of justice as preached by the world. They do not propose a bit more justice or a step nearer justice. They propose a different justice, a real reversal of priorities.

This gives me confidence in the Church: at a certain point, Christians have to ask themselves basic questions about justice, equality, freedom, and truth. They cannot help questioning the issues, even the organizations of which they are a part. They are compelled to discover the worm in the fruit and to be permanent protesters, as Christ and the Church are, at the risk of being rejected themselves. They will give voice to the silent protest of the victims. The destitute, in fact, are victims. They are made so by the very systems that are designed to insure justice but which only imply injustice for them.

Only the Church, I repeat, can carry through with this essential, global, and definitive protest. I see the Church as the only body able to impose this on the world; and I return to where we started: the Church's life is at stake here. The Church cannot help being affected in its own flesh, in its own heart, by these fallen people, these ill-treated families, and these children who live in shame at school. Because they are the Church.

To come back to your question about the ignorance of Christians: their problem is not one of being informed but of keeping themselves informed. Can they wait to be informed, or will they go and search for their own identity, for their Lord?

3.

To Be Incarnated in a People

Gilles Anouil: You do not like to criticize the Church because it is always on the path toward the destitute. But do you see any progress?

Father Joseph Wresinski: Some degree of questioning is always going on within the Church. In our times alone—during the war and a short time after it—its search has been for what we have called immersion. When I was a seminarian, many priests talked of "immersing" themselves in the masses. The ideal was to be an integral part of suffering humanity at the risk of losing oneself. This inspired me greatly, and we lived in the hope of doing so. This was for me one of the times when my life in the Church was strongest.

Are you talking about the difficult time of the war and its aftermath? Was this, then, taking place well before the time of the worker-priests?

Yes. Many people aren't aware of that part of the history of the Church. During those years, I saw priests leaving their rectories to go and live among the disadvantaged in order to be as close a neighbor to their brethren as they could.

Did they choose working-class neighborhoods?

They went to poor areas. Throughout France, I saw priests leaving everything:

42

in the Aisne region, the Paris area, and in the south. My life as a priest started in an extraordinary time. We wanted to be present among suffering people. When I asked my bishop if I could enter the Mission de France,[8] it was not to be an activist but to be in communion with a poor population. Most of us wanted to "immerse" ourselves in order to find the reality of the Church. As a side benefit, we ended up learning more about ourselves. We wanted to evangelize the poor as Christ had commanded us, while doing ourselves what Christ had already achieved: "The poor are evangelized." We believed, and I still believe, that the evangelization of the poor had already been accomplished. We wanted to go searching for the lost sheep at the risk of losing the others. We wanted to descend more deeply into suffering humanity, knowing that in this way we would find the Church in all its truth and splendor. We wanted to live our vocation in the very heart of the Church of the poor.

Was this a forerunner to the worker-priest movement?

Worker-priests did the same thing at first; they wanted both to live their vocation at the very heart of poverty and to consecrate the Eucharist nourished by the very life of suffering and distressed people. We were not talking then of a working world as we do nowadays. We did not want only to become members of the working world, but we wanted to be in communion with the world of extreme poverty.

At that time I became ill. Following my recovery, I asked my bishop for a parish where signs of extreme poverty were apparent. I expressed my wish to join a community of families, youth, and children who would be among those who suffered most. At that time a large number of us asked this of our bishops.

My diocese, Soissons, was a rural area. Bishop Douillard replied, "I haven't got what you ask for, but I can offer you a parish which, without you, would not have any priest." It was Dhuizel, a wonderful, small village of about forty homes in the Braine region. I did not know the world of farmers. However, I accepted this parish to ensure it would have a priest and also to immerse myself in it. I knew I would encounter great difficulties in this unfamiliar place. But going to Dhuizel was my way of getting close to farm workers and of sharing the hardship of their lives and work. If people knew the Church well enough, they would know that the hearts of priests are always filled with the ardent desire to join the despised and the excluded in order to share their pain and shame.

Later, in 1956, I was in complete agreement when my bishop sent me to the Noisy-le-Grand camp. I had the will "to die there" like the priests I knew in Montreuil and Ivry. In their working-class parishes, their concern was to live among a people who did not know Christ but who were calling, searching, and asking for him. Basically, we Christians are forgetful; we have already forgotten those privileged times which I had the opportunity of experiencing at the beginning of my priesthood.

Do the worker-priests remember this? According to what you say, they share this passion to become an integral part of the people.

I think so; and in my opinion, they are still searching for it. I could be mistaken, but I think they still want to go ever lower, to those depths where all the faith, hope, and charity of the Church reside. To descend to the bottom—in order to love the Church not through the poorest, but in them—is certainly the vocation of these priests, hence, their anguished need to reach unskilled workers, migrants, and victims of the worst exploitation—not to stop there, but to be always on the way, to constantly search further.

It is the Church's role to make people aware of injustice. However, it also has to be ceaselessly concerned with reaching even the poorest people, those who remain untouched, as if inaccessible, because of their great poverty. The Church knows there are always very poor people who exist, in whom Jesus Christ is embodied, and it cannot rest until it has joined them; it is condemned to going always further and deeper down.

Even today, the Church tells us that workplaces are often places of exploitation. But it reminds us that poverty also hides in other places, even lower on the social ladder, where families are without housing, resources, or recognized dignity. The Church reminds us, furthermore, that the family is the only institution to have survived the unrest of 1968 and the post-conciliar crisis. Working people await us also (and worker-priests know this well) in their homes, which are sacramental places par excellence, where God gives love and makes love grow.

And this is a great opportunity for us because in the homes, which are sometimes far from places of work, someone who has a job might be living next to someone deprived of employment. The worker-priest, by joining them in their neighborhoods, will have a chance to meet families who are unable to take part in the world of work.

In truth, our suffering and anxiety as priests might be that, at the end of our life, the Lord would tell us: "I was one of the persons in that hovel, in the emergency housing. That family paralyzed with anguish, those children deprived of schooling—that was I. You passed me by and you did not recognize me. You did not stop."

I realize, now, that you have just told your own story in the past tense: "I wanted...." But is it over?

It is not really over. Yet I dare not talk too much in the present tense because the poor have pushed me into becoming a public figure. I did not want this because I was rather ill at ease, timid, and not very sure of myself. I wanted to be a man of God, completely private, hidden, like yeast in the bread, as the Lord wanted me to be. I became a public figure against my deepest wishes. For me, a priest is the man of his people. He is close to them to the point of becoming one of them. During my first years as a priest, I was able to become profoundly absorbed in the lives of the families in my parish. Those were the happiest years of my life.

Since then, you have had to follow other roads. Has the Church made progress toward being present in the poorest areas?

Yes, certainly with regard to worker-priests devoting their lives to the most exploited workers they meet. The priests act and pray for their liberation, and if the means are sometimes surprising, we must remember that those are the only means available to the working class; such priests cannot choose other means.

But, as a whole, the priests know they cannot stop there, because the life of workers cannot be reduced to the workplace. They know they cannot ignore people's families, because the family is the last refuge for a person who is injured, mutilated, and rejected to the point of exclusion. The workers they meet also lead the priests toward neighborhood associations of which they become an integral part. They draw the priests to neighborhoods where they are more and more involved in finding different kinds of commitment and means of expression.

The priests in a working-class environment are led further for yet another reason. They discover that the world of work is not a homogeneous whole. It has a hidden side that was brought to light by the Movement—that mutilated part of its body which is the Fourth World. Jesus Christ is there, awaiting his priests. It has been said that we should be with the working class because their world is a world of hope. We all agree with this. But beyond that world, there is a world of despair where the most disadvantaged ask us for total renunciation. We can approach this world only by laying ourselves bare; we can defend it only by compromising ourselves; we can share its life only by giving it our own. Is not the world of the most disadvantaged that of love, where Christ is fully at ease because it is his own? The Church can hope for everything from this world because, like the Church itself, the most disadvantaged are not of the world and need to be delivered from evil.

Worker-priests, I am convinced, are still searching; they have not abandoned their first intuition. They go forward, and the Church goes forward with them. Today, one cannot think of the Church without priests at work. Soon these priests will also be present where people are totally deprived of work and, consequently, of their dignity as workers.

Apart from the worker-priests, are other advances being made?

In all honesty, I am not well placed to answer that because the Fourth World Movement is not a Church movement but a multi-confessional gathering of men and women. In the Church, however, I see some signs that do not deceive. I am thinking of the many priests, nuns, and laypeople who are looking to the Movement for a dialogue, for an expression by the poorest, and for a way to reach them. Their number has decreased in recent years, perhaps because our commitment is becoming increasingly public. But it might also be that they need the Movement less because they can meet the most disadvantaged in their own communities' involvement or within groups to which they belong.

The Church can make progress in many different ways, and its ways are not always those one might expect. It is not easy for those in charge of its official structures, and this has pained me at times. The Church—I am speaking here for France—is structured in a certain way, with overall pastoral policies in each diocese and specialized channels to reach the working class and provide assistance programs for the poor. The Movement situates itself below these structures, as a pre-evangelization, almost buried with a destitute people with whom we would like to surface, so that the Church would recognize itself in them. But when I say the Movement, I am thinking of countless Christians who, within it or outside it, take the plunge into the world of poverty. They are considered to be seed that dies. The Church has difficulty, sometimes, in considering these Christian people, these priests and nuns, as an integral part of itself. It does not always take the risks with them. Is this right or wrong? In any case, the Church is in an uncomfortable position, and that is understandable when one considers the structures it has imposed upon itself in order to be both of the world and able to defend itself against it.

One example of this difficulty was my experience with Secours Catholique[9] when I met with Monsignor Rodhain some twenty years ago. I was speaking of the innumerable difficulties I encountered in really getting to know the poorest families in order to join in their struggle, or sometimes just in trying to get enough to eat myself.

I added that seeing me share their sufferings this way was probably of value for the families, but that not all committed people like myself should have to go through this. Some of the hardships were pointless, and I expressed my wish that the Secours Catholique would come to the aid of those who were sacrificing their health and their lives in emergency housing camps, shantytowns, and gray, dirty slum areas. Apart from material means, these men and women also needed a solid body of knowledge. Could the SC become a source of knowledge about the destitute? Could it not, at least, offer these committed men and women the material means that were sadly lacking and which they obtained by asking for private contributions? In this way, SC could act as coordinator and support group for those who responded to the appeals of the persons who suffered most. Nothing came of this, and there were many who continued to live on the edge and exhaust themselves in order to draw the poorest out of their condition. I felt much pain in seeing them forced, as I was, to permanently beg for the means to go on with their work. This would lead us, later on, to create the Science and Service Clubs that would support them.

But if the Church did not support us within its structures, it did not attempt to repossess us either. It respected us too much. One day, Cardinal Marty reminded me of this: "You wanted to create a movement where men and women of all denominations could gather around the poorest. The best way of helping you was to accept this from the start and to let you go on your way." It is correct to say that the Church has never doubted our sincerity and has never ceased to trust us.

When you were a young priest, then, the Church never tried to stop you. Wasn't it worried when it saw you battling with public authorities?

The Church preached caution and patience to the priests and laity scattered in poor areas. I told you that these were more numerous than we thought, as poverty is always a focal point for the gathering of people. They open up, seek to understand and liberate. Those who encounter extreme poverty do not always do what is necessary; however they are marked for life. Rare are those who do not become committed to justice and peace. Rest assured that the Church was not indifferent to their efforts, but it gave them freedom so they could fully share the lives of the destitute. Of course, we would like the Church to be more active and closer to those who try to reach families at the heart of extreme poverty. These people sometimes despair at the apparent pointlessness of their efforts.

Are there really so many of them outside your Movement? Why do we not hear about them?

I do not know of one poor area where people are not already involved. Unfortunately, they remain unknown. They are, however, witnesses and agents of our common commitment. Public opinion in France, which is ill-informed, eventually equated the struggle against poverty to the Fourth World Movement. This is wrong. The Movement certainly has a specific way of seeing the poor and some original things to say. It has given them back their history and, thanks to it, their dignity can no longer be denied. And many people outside the Movement are inspired by it.

In your view, is the Fourth World Movement carrying an original message in the larger attempt to become one with very poor people?

The Movement arose from a very strong intuition at its very beginnings in the Noisy-le-Grand camp. It was then that I became clearly aware that the families gathered there should not be seen as individuals side by side, or a cluster of individual cases, of "social cases," as the administration and the charitable organizations believed then and still believe too often. The Movement knew from the start that they represented a whole people. It is, therefore, in and for a people that the Movement grew. To see a people when everyone saw "social cases," to see a historical identity where others were denying that this was a social reality—all this amounted to making reference to the people of Israel and their long march in the desert. Walking alongside a poverty-stricken people, we wanted to place them boldly in the pages of today's history. We rejected the fact that history has not dealt with their existence. We refused to see them treated as individual cases, and we asserted the existence of a people living in the shadow of modern society. In order to proclaim this historical reality as part of our effort for the liberation of the Fourth World, we had to develop new ways of thinking and acting.

You say "we" or "the Movement." Didn't you found the Movement?

Others did so with me. The initial step was mine; it was the result of the shock I experienced upon my arrival at Noisy-le-Grand. Even though I had been brought up in poverty myself and I have seen many poor areas since, Noisy-le-Grand was like a revelation.

My bishop had proposed that I spend some time among these destitute families and then choose whether I wanted to stay with them. I went there for six months at first and, for the first month and a half, I was associated with the Companions of Emmaus. I worked with them, I lived like them and, as they were doing repair work at the Noisy-le-Grand camp, I was able to approach families living there.

I arrived on the plateau called "Le Château de France" on the fourteenth of July, 1956. The sun was scorching and the alleys were deserted. There was no one outside. In front of this emptiness, I said to myself, "In the old days, sources of water, road junctions, churches, or businesses brought people together. Here, utter poverty is what brings people together." This was like an inspiration. I knew I was not facing a usual situation of relative poverty (as one would say then) or personal problems. I had to deal with collective extreme poverty. I felt at once that I was in the presence of my people. I cannot explain it. That is how it was.

From that moment, my own life took a turn. Because, on that day, I vowed that if I stayed, I would see to it that one day these families could go to the Vatican, the Elysée Palace, and the UN. The blinding poverty that lay before me in stifling heat and absolute silence had me caught in a trap. Since then, I have been haunted by the idea that those people would never escape from their poverty as long as they were not welcomed as a whole, as a people, in those places where other people held debates or led struggles. They had to be there, on equal terms, in every place where people discuss and make decisions not only about the present, but also about people's destiny and the future of humanity.

On July 14, 1956, I sealed my fate, even if I waited until November to settle for good in Noisy-le-Grand. Even on that day, the eleventh of November, I still held on to my old parish. I kept going there every Saturday and Sunday.

Born as a child in deep poverty and having remained a man of poverty, I had learned to believe in everything, to dare anything, but still to keep something in reserve somewhere—put something away for a rainy day, a stale piece of bread in my pocket. There is not one poor person who would not do likewise. My own mother would keep a spare pair of shoes for her children, or a spare pair of trousers. When someone brought us another pair of secondhand shoes—we did get many handouts—my mother would say to the benefactor, "Thank goodness you came. It's just what we needed." When we were on our own, I would ask her, "Mama, why did you do all that play-acting?" She would tell me, "Joseph, you don't understand. If you refuse what they bring you today, the day you do need something they will have given it away to someone else." I kept my old parish for several months as a security measure, like my mother who always kept an extra pair of shoes.

You had much audacity, took many risks, and yet you always kept that habit "to put something away for a rainy day."

It is a pauper's habit. It is a fear, a dread of having to go without. You cannot get out of it. It is a wisdom that guides you throughout your life. I never spent a penny that was not mine. Everything we built in the Movement was done on a day-to-day basis, even if that meant leaving a work site unattended for three years running. I was never able to invest anything we did not have in our pockets. We poor people always have to beat misfortune by several lengths. To lack something is the essence of our condition, and if by chance we have the bare necessities, we still have, deep down, the fear of being without means.

But finally, you did manage to cast off the moorings and belong entirely in the Fourth World?

True; but the Movement that came into existence learned caution from the destitute. By embracing the conditions of a people, it also embraced their way of behaving and their wisdom.

4.

Fourth World, People of God

Gilles Anouil: Let us now talk about this people. You, yourself, have called it the Fourth World. In France there are more than two million people in this World, and according to you, they constitute a people. This is not obvious or even credible in the eyes of many French.

Father Joseph Wresinski: It is no doubt difficult for many people to understand the poorest people taken as a whole, to identify the people through its history and its own experience of life transmitted from one generation to the next, as is often the case. In the first place the difficulty, perhaps, stems from the fact that in order to identify a population which apparently is an integral part of our own society, we need to discover in it some similar features, some signs of kinship. Then we can form bonds and begin to interact. But families at the bottom of the social ladder experience such a degree of underdevelopment that their fellow citizens are no longer able to identify with them; therefore they do not consider themselves responsible for the condition of these families. They do not even think they have anything to do with them. This is why the underprivileged remain so alien to our societies.

You say "our societies." Do you mean European societies?

I mean the Western world in general; that is to say, probably all industrialized societies, all those that have forgotten the existence of extreme poverty within their frontiers.

Besides, irresponsibility in the affluent leads to the same attitude of irresponsibility in the poorest. The underprivileged themselves are not aware of partaking in the history of others; therefore, they do not think they share any responsibility for this history today. They behave as if they formed a world of their own. To approach them really means to approach a strange, surprising, incomprehensible world. This is true as regards sensibilities: outsiders do not see how they could feel any concern for what these families live and even less for how they live. The more so because these families seem to keep on thwarting outsiders.

Let us not forget that the underprivileged, because of their history and their living conditions, do not possess the same wisdom as we do. Theirs is a different wisdom, leading to a different behavior. The cohesion of their culture is not the same as ours, even if the basic elements are identical. Their actions cannot be analyzed from the point of view of any history other than their own. Take the example of a family housed in an absolutely unspeakable type of accommodation, such as a shed, a garage, or an old truck. Somebody decides to get them out of it and spares no effort to find them decent accommodation. This person goes so far as to antagonize his friends, and he agrees to be guarantor. Just as everything seems to be settled, the family refuses to budge. They almost insult that person, telling him they never asked him for anything. Or, in another case, the family might disappear without a word of warning.

The man of goodwill is left stranded with a dwelling on his hands and his own prestige in jeopardy, with everybody telling him, "We told you so." As for the family, they had their own reasons. They had no experience of that type of accommodation and they vaguely sensed that new problems were in store for them: for example, a rent to pay, new surroundings with inquisitive neighbors, inevitable confrontations with a caretaker, loss of the few old friendships they had, or the breaking up of the aid network they relied on. It is difficult for a society with a certain cultural heritage concerning housing and life with neighbors, to realize what it means not to have received the same heritage. When we move a family as impoverished as this, we do not imagine we are tearing apart an already infinitely delicate social fabric, a fabric all the more precious because it is so thin. The ultimate risk is that we may also tear apart its family fabric. As a result of such uprooting, I have seen fathers leave jobs that were obtained after much trouble and mothers take up with another partner.

To anyone not acquainted with this social group, all this is incomprehensible. Had not this family been on the move many times before? Yes, surely; they had gone from furnished accommodations to a cellar, from a cellar to an attic, from a trailer to a tent, from a hovel to a shack. But in the course of all these moves (a hard thing to realize), they never left their social group. It was from the same social group that they were able to get addresses and the means to go from one place to the next. By interfering from outside, we cut them off from their own world and transplanted them into another, where relationships are based on a different type of contract.

I have seen such displaced families treat as a hostage the person who had rehoused them. They kept relying on this person, asking for his help again and again, and when they met the least refusal, they would denigrate him. This is only one example of the disconcerting relationships that exist between two worlds and that discourage any person of goodwill or any disinterested approach. People thought they were dealing with a family from their own world, experiencing temporary difficulty. But while they intended to strengthen the family's security, they had, in fact, been destroying it. If people are not aware of this, sooner or later they will accuse those they tried to help, saying, "There is nothing we can do with such people!" This is not a rash statement. It is the result of the experience of a whole society that has allowed some of its own to be lost on the road of exclusion. It no longer knows how to be united with them; its attempts at doing so are clumsy. Unfortunately, the price of such clumsiness is not paid by society. Once they have been disappointed, people of goodwill have many opportunities to recover; their prestige and their feeling of security were never really at stake. Poor families, on the other hand, have no reserves; they end up a little more rejected, a little more damaged than before.

I still find it difficult to see these families as belonging to a specific group. I have met destitute families who are isolated and do not know anyone. Do they really constitute a people?

Our eyes can deceive us. These families have been tossed about, displaced, scattered to the four winds, and herded together again only to be scattered once more, according to the way our cities and towns evolve and to the vagaries of town and country planning. You would be surprised to discover how, in spite of everything, they manage to keep in touch, maintaining relationships that we fail to notice most of the time. First and foremost there are family ties, for they tend to marry within their own circles. For instance, a young man will marry his neighbor's daughter or his fellow worker's sister. Then there are relationships that result from living in the same neighborhood, from having spent one's childhood in the same slum area. Not to mention their common history; that is, having been through the same experience of underemployment, social aid, eviction, and children placed in foster care; and having similar experiences of shortcomings, illness, or hunger. Fourth World families may quarrel frequently, but they never break with their past. They never cut off their moorings for good. I have never known very poor families living in total isolation. They can always fall back on existing relationships with their own kin, with families like their own, and with people representing the various aid organizations—"nice people," as they say.

We get the wrong idea when we watch these families from a distance, but, at the same time, they mislead us. When tens or even hundreds of them live in the same housing complex, they tend to be the first to criticize their surroundings. The neighborhood serves as a pretext or excuse vis-à-vis the outside world: "If my kids don't learn anything at school, it's because the teachers resent people from our block. My children are not exceptions; none of the children from down here learn anything. It's the teacher's fault. He doesn't like us, which is not surprising. Just look at the people who live here; they're all good-for-nothings."

Whenever there is a fight or a crime in the housing complex, the neighbors are used as scapegoats: "The good and the bad are to be found here, as anywhere else." "You see, these people are no good." In any case, in order to ingratiate themselves with social workers or town officials, the families have no alternative but to keep their distance from the disreputable neighborhood: "I don't actually belong here. If I'm here, it's only because of bad luck." By denying their belonging to this social group, they in fact say that they could be part of it, that it does exist. But such betrayal is necessary, inevitable, and constant. In this, Fourth World people are always like Peter: "I do not know this man." But they are also children of God, constantly betrayed by their brothers and sisters, by the people on whom they have a right to rely.

However, behind this betrayal, a secret, obscure, invisible, and unsuspected life is hidden. For even when we are close to them, the families never tell us everything. Strangers in their own country, their groups formed as the result of more or less fortuitous and in any case unfortunate circumstances—or so we believe. They tell us only what they have decided to reveal, what will serve their interests. They disclose only what they deem vital for their survival against all odds. Their mutual relationships are an asset they keep for themselves as much as possible. They do not acknowledge them, for they know we would try to break them. They are used to hearing people say to them, "Of course, as long as you keep company with those individuals who lead you into drinking or betting on horses...." In other words, "Birds of a feather flock together." Poor families are well acquainted with such remarks, and they do their utmost to avoid them.

As I was telling you before, we hardly know the reality of life for the underprivileged; the face they show us is too disfigured, and we find it difficult to establish bonds of friendship and mutual understanding with them. The more we try, the more we ensnare ourselves in the mesh of our refusal to acknowledge their existence as a people. To do so would amount to an avowal of our guilt. Therefore, we do our best to prevent the manifestation of this people as a separate social entity. Indeed, our failure to understand becomes a refusal to understand, and we deny its existence. Instead of recognizing the unique milieu of the poorest and using it as a springboard for their own liberation, instead of accepting their values lived out day to day, we claim to protect each family from the others, thus breaking up the people into isolated cases. The families know this, and they play the game. They keep secret a part of their life of neighborliness, mutual aid, and sharing. Let us be wary of well-meaning but deluded people who tell us, "I know everything about this family. They tell me everything. We are friends." It is never quite true. This family, whose whole story is supposedly known, has too high a sense of its own dignity and of others to disclose everything.

The same applies to those of us who share their lives and live in the same housing projects and slum neighborhoods. Some families had me believing inaccurate things for many years. For instance, for fifteen years a woman had me believing that she had no relatives and had been brought up in state institutions where nuns used to beat her. She gave all the details and the names of the institutions. (Underprivileged families know these as a part of their world.) This woman made herself out to be another person in order to survive in a society that had deprived her of her own children.

How did you learn this was untrue? How did you discover what others had failed to see?

By sharing their daily lives. The mother in question wanted me to help her get her children back. Together we reconstructed her life story in order to justify her request. One thing led to another, and we discovered she had spent all her childhood with her parents. Her father was a day-laborer going from farm to farm. Hers was a large and deprived family leading a life of exclusion; they were not liked by the townspeople. The children were rejected in school, and the family had no link with the Church. When the woman was still very young, she married a young man from the area, to escape her unbearable life. He was a carpenter's son. It proved to be an impossible union: the husband and wife could not get along. The whole village turned against this woman from a family it held in contempt, the woman who had dared to marry a respectable young man.

The woman finally eloped with another man from her own social background, and the couple ended up in a run-down housing project. For fifteen years they lived there through ups and downs, exchanging blows and insults, experiencing hunger, and having their children taken away from them. Yet she loved her second husband right to the end, looking after him for many months with maternal concern. She never complained about him, for he understood her. However, when confronted by the social services, she had to invent a bogus identity, pretending to have been in the care of the state and to have been ill-treated as a child. That was an easy thing to do, since the Fourth World is teeming with such situations.

For that matter, I have known several young women who, when they were seventeen or so, married young working men in order to escape, not from their family but from their social environment. Such unions nearly always turn out badly, except when the young man becomes integrated into the environment from which his wife wanted to escape. When separation occurs, the children are usually put in foster care, and the woman starts life again with someone who shares her sensitivity and lifestyle. This explains why family bonds are so complex and unclear in the housing projects. But they also serve as proof—and the fate of these women is one example—of the existence of a specific social background and of a people, that is, a people bound by a secret communion that enables the men and women to know each other without many words being spoken, to live their lives together for their own sake and that of their children.

Actually, under present circumstances, crossing over to the other side and becoming part of the working class is not possible unless one finds the strength to break away from one's kin for good. In order to do that, people need sound reasons. I myself know of only a few examples, such as that of a young woman who, by marrying a worker who was an active member of the communist workers' union, became a communist activist herself. As a party member, she was able to re-evaluate her previous situation and stop being ashamed of herself. But such examples are rare; the great majority of young people from the Fourth World marry their own.

You said that the underprivileged possess a wisdom different from ours. What about mutual aid and solidarity? Do they set a model to be followed, then?

By wisdom, I meant a strategy for everyday life, a way of keeping one's options open. For example, I know of one family who escaped to avoid being moved to a housing project for which they felt no affinity.

But what can be said of mutual aid and solidarity within the Fourth World? We all practice the kind of solidarity we can afford, according to our own interest. Christians, however, know that their solidarity must embrace every single person, even to sacrificing oneself, since as a child of God, each person is sacred. Unfortunately, this same society crams people together so that it is very difficult to personally welcome one's neighbors or to form a significant relationship with them. Victims of overcrowding, unknown to each other and interchangeable, are forced to choose neighbors from among an anonymous crowd.

Neighbors are no longer those whom life places at your side; they are persons you choose for yourself. This is a serious privation about which modern society shows little foresight, because people usually grow by rubbing shoulders with others who are different from them. We are enriched by strangers, persons we did not know, who through daily interchanges teach us who they are and what they think. We grow richer by expending ourselves through the aid we offer to a neighborhood we have not chosen. But modern society does not facilitate such relationships with neighbors, or the solidarity it entails.

On the other hand, no choice is possible when one lives in an underprivileged environment. The person next door is as much in need as you are. Will your generosity be greater because of this? Indeed, it will be all the more difficult to practice, since in a world of destitution it is nearly impossible to be completely disinterested. Giving becomes a vital necessity. How could you not do it, since one day you will need your neighbor's help? How could you refuse to give today, since you will be at the receiving end tomorrow? Helping in the Fourth World is always with the provision that something will be done in return at another time.

My mother, poor as she was, lived on very good terms with the woman next door, who was equally poor. Unfortunately, this lady drank. Often when her son came home in the evening, he found his mother in a state of collapse, with no dinner ready. My mother then used to take him in to share our meal, understanding that she could count on that neighbor in her own time of need. I could almost say that my mother found it hard to forgive that woman for the service she did for the son. She sometimes took revenge by declaring out loud to her own children, "When I think of the good I do for her when Maxime is hungry...."

Throughout the world of the poor, I have encountered this difficulty in accepting that the other person relies on your support. The reason is that giving means drawing from basic necessities of life, really doing without. This entails extra hardship and brings on reproaches from husband, children, and social services. You feel as if you have behaved badly toward your own family.

Yet, sometimes the poor surprise us by a generosity verging on munificence. For instance, when the garbagemen and the firemen call for their New Year's gift, or when the mailman brings a money order, poor persons might hand over an amount of money that seems a fortune to them. Similarly, these persons will give a large sum to a neighbor collecting money for a funeral. But is that a sign of solidarity? Is it not rather an ill-placed gesture to gain some acknowledgment, some respect? It is, indeed, a way of playing the role of a lord. Of course, there is no real calculated move in that, and the poor do not necessarily regret this munificence if they can enjoy being "someone" for a brief moment. There is more to it: they also want to prove they were workers themselves and they understand the working man—the garbageman, the mailman, the man who has a job. As you can see, it is very difficult to be disinterested in such circumstances. Being destitute does not lead to real sharing nor does it promote solidarity.

Does this difficulty in sharing also apply to feeling affection for or listening to the other person?

The reason we desperately fight against poverty and utterly reject it, is probably because it creates a situation of inferiority and deprivation in which listening to each other is made impossible. We intuitively perceive this—the underprivileged guess what others feel but they do not really hear them. Words are scarce; vocabulary is inadequate. How, then, could they have real dialogues? Without the ability to really talk to one another, they cannot build a common way of thinking. As early as thirty or thirty-five, men are often worn out, looking almost like old men. The necessity of solving immediate problems, of facing up to the need for food, money, or housing takes up all the resources of one's intelligence and thinking. Can you imagine what goes through the mind of a person who is always short of money, living in anguish, wondering all the time how the kids will be fed and clothed and how to respond to their request for that toy or ice cream? The poorest have to face up to such demands from the children—they want a candy or a piece of clothing, for example. Let us try to imagine what it means for them in terms of anxiety, of having to calculate how to meet basic needs or how to prepare a meal when there is no food left in the house and the husband threatens to stay home from work if he doesn't have a packed lunch to take. "And if he doesn't go to work, there'll be fighting at home."

One's spirit is worn out, one's thoughts go round in circles. What can one do except act stupid? So if an expected sum of money comes in, all of it will be spent at once, in reaction to anguish and hunger. The neighbors who gave money when food was short are paid back. The table, bare for too long when the purse was empty, will be piled up with foods they could only dream of before; for example, red meat, chicken, savory sausage, strawberries, costly early fruit or vegetables. Social workers will then say these families are incapable of planning, of saving, and of managing a budget. They forget that these people constantly worry about such things as how to pay the rent or buy school lunches. Under such circumstances, how could a person who is always restless and misunderstood show any interest in other people's preoccupations and ideas? Poor families guess the suffering of the other person, they feel empathy and are genuinely moved, but this empathy can never last more than a brief moment. In the Fourth World, the families are indeed able, as nobody else, to share the other person's grief. But this does not lead to solidarity or sustained mutual aid. Such mutual aid between the poorest exists, but only sporadically and as a response at a given time. As soon as the situation changes and the respite has passed, antagonistic attitudes take over once more. After giving help extravagantly and generously, people will destroy one another with the same lack of measure. Clashes and denunciations will crop up again: "We don't speak to those people any more. They've caused us too much trouble."

Creating a common history within the Fourth World is a difficult thing. Families live their part of history; they endure it, but they have no grip on it. A part of history begun in friendship is gradually undermined. Because of the impossibility of sharing ideas, of communicating, and of planning ahead, the

Fourth World is a universe in which people are bound only by their extreme poverty. There will always come a time when people are irritated and exasperated. Then they suspect one another, lose confidence, and accuse one another. Sometimes these clashes are real; other times people find an excuse for a dispute, while the true cause is the lack of physical and moral stamina for the pursuit of a common project. For instance, several people resolved to go to the town hall together or to go in a group and meet a school principal. But, when the time comes, they are all at a loss to face the mayor without embarrassment or to know how to address the principal.

Their experience has taught them that they are the weakest anyway, that they are always wrong. Why, then, go to the town hall or the school? To justify their abdication, they will allege their neighbors' duplicity. What other reason could they put forward, if not that their neighbors are dishonest and only seek their own interest? This is not always true, yet unfortunately they are often right.

Could not this abdication be explained by their inability to imagine a better world? I remember a story you wrote about a man who, after having fixed up his home, smashed it to pieces with an axe.

The man was just out of prison, in a state of euphoria. From that moment on, he thought, everything would be all right. He had started to install a sink with a cabinet underneath. He had been welcomed by his wife and given some money by a neighbor, and he thought, "A new life is starting." Then, one night, quarrels began again. His wife, no longer used to his presence, criticized him about something. He got hold of an axe and smashed everything. When he returned from prison, he had believed that change was possible; he would have liked to tell his wife and children that he, too, had changed. He missed one little sign of tenderness, and that had been enough to make him break the work of his own hands and humiliate his wife and children. He felt despair at finding that life was still the same, and he thought, "I was a fool, doing it all for her; she really doesn't deserve it."

The impossibility of establishing and maintaining trusting relationships between people, between husband and wife, defeats all efforts. Even the intimate life of married couples is permanently disturbed because of the difficulties of building a life together. What hope is there, then, of being on friendly terms with the people around you? Had not one neighbor given the sink and another, the paint? For a brief moment, it seemed, an understanding had been created within the family, and things had also been going well within the immediate neighborhood. But when everything is shattered, who among us can understand? We are only confirmed in our opinion that a person must be stupid to help such people, that they don't want to change, and that their wretchedness is of their own making. How can we perceive, behind their broken lives, the painful progression of a whole people?

Is this common fate a sufficient explanation for the transmission of extreme poverty from generation to generation, as you have described it?

Indeed, the feeling of being unrecognized and never achieving anything is transmitted from generation to generation. But a situation is passed on from one generation to the next in the Fourth World because the surrounding world recreates the same lack of understanding, the same rejection, with each new generation. The basis of this is a judgment with serious repercussions passed on from age to age by public opinion. Public opinion considers poor families incapable of reason and willpower, of affection for their children, of any desire to change, and even of spirituality.

Yet—and I can vouch for this—the underprivileged would like to believe and pray, not as a matter of giving up but of strengthening their hope. Since they are always put in the wrong and made ashamed of their own failures, they want to believe in a God of mercy and forgiveness. And we, systematically ignoring their surges of energy and their efforts on each other's behalf, and blaming them all the time for their lack of human qualities, make them weaker still and introduce meanness into their lives. We hinder them from believing in a good and forgiving God. If there were an ounce of humanity in us, we would admit that we are personally responsible for ruining the best in them because of the life we impose on them. We have confined them within the mediocrity of poor housing, unhealthy jobs, and pathetic wages. We have denied them the means of leading decent lives and of allowing solidarity, esteem, and trust to develop between families. When shall we understand that the first right we have to acknowledge is their right to forgiveness?

Fourth World families are in constant need of forgiveness, but society is sparing of this commodity. It never forgets, and it prosecutes them for years for petty crimes, denying them any chance of mending their ways. This does not facilitate forgiveness between families, either. And yet, crammed as they are in housing projects, living in anguish, always on the lookout, and constantly experiencing disappointment in each other, these families cannot possibly survive if they do not forgive one another. Their lives teach us that the right to forgiveness is also the right to be able to forgive one's neighbor. Otherwise, how can they go on living side by side? But, on the other hand, how can one forgive when one is reminded at every moment of the conflicts, the quarrels, and the break-ups, when children fight each other, and a neighbor disturbs the night with an infernal row?

Today more than ever, we consider it difficult to turn to God. On my part, I testify that the poorest are on the way to God, perhaps more so than others are, because of their thirst for absolution. But for them to believe it, the Church has to tell them and accept them. To do this, the Church needs to relearn everything about mercy and forgiveness. The Church no longer demonstrates—and it's a pity—that confession is not only a sacrament of purification but also a reminder of the tenderness of God for God's children, an act that affirms God's forgiveness.

What you say here contradicts the current idea that the poor have a right to judge their oppressors, for I assume they cannot be penitent and judge at the same time. Are you not taking the risk of being criticized for reversing the order of priorities in the liberation of the poor?

It is for the poorest, not for us, to decide what the priorities are. Their whole lives are an appeal for mercy: "I didn't mean to hit my wife... I didn't want to scold my husband... I didn't want to admit that my son was a thief... And yet I did it." They are always thinking, "Is it my fault? Tell me it can't possibly be my fault."

Let me tell you about our experience when we started a legal aid office in a shantytown of the Paris region. The legal advisers in our Movement had wanted to open an office to advise people about their rights. The overwhelming reactions of the families of "La Campa" shantytown dissuaded them from doing so. They flocked to the office for months on end and asked for help to put themselves straight with the authorities. People would say: "I stole tires for my car," "I'm driving without a license," "I cashed a postal order I wasn't entitled to," "I lied to my boss," or "I emptied my neighbor's letter box." Petty crimes, you will say, but these were only the tip of the iceberg. It was their way of telling us they wanted above all to be true to their own values.

You might ask what right I have to be so positive about their desire to make things right with God. True, in the past the poorest seldom came to the confessional. Today they probably do so even less frequently. However, at times when families were being reconciled, I have seen one person or another linger in my office to tell me, after a time, "It's ten or twenty years since I went to confession." And they would kneel down. Christ, who knows people's hearts well, never met the poor without granting them forgiveness as well as healing them or giving them bread. And all the people who have really contributed to the advancement of the poor have first liberated the poor from themselves. They have given the poor back their dignity and restored their trust in themselves. They believed in them and persuaded them they were not responsible for a wretchedness inherited from history.

You asked me a question about the transmission of extreme poverty. Researchers in the social sciences have talked about it for the last thirty years; books have been published about the habits and the ways of thinking of the poor, as well as about the language transmitted among them. Basically, the poorest pass on from generation to generation the belief that they are responsible for their situation—a belief that is kept alive by society. They find it very hard to rise above this belief, since they keep committing acts of which they themselves disapprove. Living in contradiction to their own convictions leads to their inability to live and love which is transmitted from parents to children through events experienced together.

One eleven-year-old girl confessed to me one morning in tears, "You know, Father, last night my father wanted to sleep with my mother again, but she didn't want to. They argued and fought, so to make him leave my mother alone, I took an empty can lying on the table and threw it in his face. He came after me. I ran away through the camp, and he chased after me for a long time. When he came back, he was very tired and had no more desire to sleep with my mother. Now she won't have another baby."

Nearly all Fourth World children could tell similar stories which tie people together in the same chaotic life, where everything is lived in the open: conflicts and marital relationships, love and hatred, grief and hope. I remember another young girl, an eight-year-old, who regularly came to see me with a note from her mother asking for money. One day it got on my nerves, and I sent her away saying, "Go back to your mother and tell her to come herself if she wants something." The child went away, but she turned around, looked at me, and said, "What about me, Father, do I have the right to eat?"

This is an example of a kind of blackmail for survival in which children are involved together with adults. They also share the deep and half-conscious feeling of suffering an injustice. Many things are left untold, but they are experienced by every person through daily happenings. This was the case of a girl I knew when she was seven and whom I watched grow up. Today she is married and a mother of two. When she was a child, she wore old clothes donated by charities. One day, I found her looking after and pampering her newborn brother lying on a pile of cardboard. She had wrapped an old jacket around him. How many other young girls just like her wrap up their newborn siblings lying on packing cardboard or old clothes, which serve as mattresses for the poor? I have just seen the very same picture in a family of northern France, who have been prosecuted for mistreating their children. It was the same incredible image of distress but viewed as if the parents had committed an offense!

And so, poverty is transmitted through events experienced together, through ill-fitting and worn-out clothes, through objects and situations— both children and adults playing the roles that such situations imply. This reflects the transmission of misery but also of a struggle for survival. For poor people do not give up easily, especially where children are concerned. Even when parents can no longer do anything because they are paralyzed by cold, fright, and anxiety, the children keep going, if only to steal from a supermarket. Perhaps for less deprived children stealing is wrong. But it is altogether different when one is in search of rice or pasta to feed a whole family. Here, they are participating in a struggle for survival. To recognize their struggle would amount to a form of forgiveness, but who recognizes such heroic efforts?

A few days ago, somewhere in France, three children from an underprivileged family were arrested for stealing some packages of pasta and rice. They had also bitten into a bar of chocolate without taking it away. They had only taken the bare necessities. They were put into state care. Yet, in these circumstances, stealing indicated a sense of responsibility: "I had to bring food to my mother." Here again, the experiences of parents and children are inextricably mingled. Adults have to take youngsters everywhere with them because they do not want to leave them on their own at home, where they are likely to cause mischief or maybe burn themselves on the stove. A woman told me the other day, "I started life on my mother's shoulder when I was one-and-a-half years old, and she had to go to court because she had stolen a hundred francs to feed us." She couldn't possibly have remembered this episode, but throughout her childhood, similar events must have caused her mother to say, "For us, things have always turned out badly. My daughter wasn't yet two when I had to carry her in my arms to go to court."

Participating with their parents in contacts with neighbors, as well as with the outside world, has an impact on children. The social worker, the pediatric nurse, the people who come to read the gas, electricity, or water meter—all these people behave in a certain way toward the parents. They see the way the household is kept, the way the children are dressed, and the way they speak. The children feel that these people are not their friends. Not that they are necessarily enemies either; but they are people from another world who come into their homes, usually making life more miserable by showering their parents with advice, demanding from them money they don't have, and asking them to explain why they have not done what they have been told to do. Maybe the mother did not follow instructions for fear of being humiliated, or she did not fill in that form because she could hardly write. The social worker who then asks her to fill in the form will notice that the woman can't write. The child, who is privy to everything, feels the shame of it: "Mama cried because she had to write in front of the social worker but she can't. Mama had to say, 'Look, Germaine, do it for me,' and then she was ashamed and after the social worker had gone, she cried."

This is how a people is formed, with its own way of life, its own language, its own understanding of events and relationships with other people. The most overwhelming feeling of all, nurtured by the environment, is that of being guilty: "You don't know, but you ought to know...." "You're not doing, but you ought to do...." People spend hours in line waiting, only to be criticized when reaching the counter: "Ah yes, it's you. You're the one whose husband has a drinking problem, aren't you?" or "Another child? Haven't you heard of the pill?" There have been occasions when I have waited for hours with parents and, when our turn came, the clerk ignored them as if they did not exist. The clerk would make a point of talking only to me. And the mother was lucky if she was not told, "You decided to keep the child then. What's the point? Children are easily adopted nowadays." For an allowance of a few hundred francs, a clerk will say, "Do you realize how much you cost those who work for a living?"

In the old days, the poor were said to be dirty: "They don't know how to wash." I, myself, heard this remark as a child. Today we hear, "They don't even know how to use the pill." This was also said in my mother's time, behind her back. They said this because she had five children, four of whom were still alive. But today they say it to people's faces and in front of the children: "You should be thinking seriously of having an abortion." The remarks I heard about my mother when I was a child are still in my memory and in my heart. Children today do not forget, either. They always retain that predominant feeling of being guilty, of having committed wrongdoing that will never be forgiven.

Yet, behind this feeling of guilt is a people belonging to a social group with its own moral standards. This morality has been transmitted from parents to children, which should make us respect them. For through this common experience, which seems to us devoid of education, a code of ethics is transmitted. Modesty is passed on from parents to children. Crude expressions hide a real sensitivity, a moral cleanliness, and a feeling of self-respect. Thefts do not undermine respect for other people's private property. Necessity does not annihilate values, it only leads to a bending of rules, which causes shame. Such is the infernal situation resulting from extreme poverty: "We should like to be different but there is no hope. And yet our honor would oblige us to start anew."

This need is transmitted within families from one generation to the next, even to children who hardly knew their parents. I am thinking of all those who have been put into the care of the state. Not long ago, I had the opportunity of meeting at least seven Fourth World families who live in this area, scattered around Pontoise. In five of them, one or both of the parents had worked on farms as wards of the state. These families all knew each other—two were even related—yet the social services treated them as isolated cases.

As I have said before, their common history and relationships form them into a people, uniting them and tearing them apart at the same time. The main factor that binds them together is the common feeling of being guilty, the hunger for forgiveness, and the certainty, buried deep in their consciousness, of being the victims of injustice.

It has been my conviction for a long time that the Church has a duty to listen to this appeal for forgiveness from the poorest. As God's people, they are on a path leading to God. They would turn to the Church if it were willing to understand and to forgive. Is this not the essential mission given by Christ: "What you forgive on earth will also be forgiven in heaven." The Fourth World expects no more from the Church than this assurance of being cleansed. The unbroken chain of humiliations, experienced as so many misdeeds and so many unperformed duties, constitutes all the difference between extreme poverty and a poverty that is merely material and relative. It is also the difference between a society that is merely unfair and one that is definitely cruel. I sometimes wonder to what extent we are able to measure the distance between the two. On the side of relative poverty, you can see situations in which exploited victims can at least denounce the injustice done to them: "I am underpaid, I am unemployed. Here are the ill effects of capitalism and of employers' greed." But, in extreme poverty you see a complete oppression, one which is being justified and about which nothing can be done: "You know very well that one cannot do anything for these people." Misery is not just being inferior because one has been deprived of power; it is the maiming of one's basic nature as a human being. The underprivileged are treated as inferior in every respect and considered sub-human. So much so that, even in this time of crisis, they are accused of being unemployed. Among the very poor, 60 percent of the adult population is without a job. Other unemployed workers benefit from our solidarity and our struggles. Underprivileged workers are not even treated with courtesy in employment offices. It is said of them, "They have no skills and, in any case, they don't like to work. They're lazy, that's what they are." Can you imagine a situation nowadays in which an unemployed person is obliged to apologize for being out of work, obliged to ask people at the unemployment office to be forgiven for that?

5.

Where Do They Come From?

Gilles Anouil: You have just mentioned disadvantaged workers and unemployment. We shall return to the question of the job situation in the Fourth World, but you stress the importance of knowing the past in order to understand today's situations.

Father Joseph Wresinski: Yes; I would like to discuss the job situation among Fourth World people, because they are part of the work force. Even if extreme poverty has left its mark on them, they cannot be denied their place in the working world. But I agree with you: we must talk about their whole history before speaking of their job history.

For centuries, extreme poverty has been part of Western societies. We know this thanks to people who, in every period of history, sought to bring relief to the poor. We may not know the history of the victims, but at least we know that of their champions. Through the testimonies of people who defended the poor, we know that extreme poverty has taken many forms. Sometimes the poorest were found wandering, uprooted, vagabonds; sometimes they were in groups joined together by the demands of the road. At times, they were spread over the countryside, in hunger and silence. And at other times, they were piled up in overcrowded, noisy, unhealthy urban areas.

What should we know about the reasons for such destitution? For the purpose of our discussion, I think we can make the following points. In all ages, whether in times of shortage or in times of plenty, the most destitute have always paid the price of progress and of regression, and the price of the catastrophes affecting their contemporaries. We mentioned earlier the intermingling, the scattering and regrouping of families in separate housing projects, as practiced today. Such enforced rehousing is the price paid by these families for better urban amenities for others. Before that, they were blamed for the deterioration of some districts and were driven back into the vilest hovels, cellars, or attics. In this way, the price of urbanization, whether for better or worse, has always been paid by the poorest. The growth and enrichment of cities, from the Middle Ages and even before, has taken place at their expense. There was a time when they were ordered to leave the city before nightfall and before the closing of the gates. There were times when they were shut up in asylums and homes for the elderly, in workhouses and poorhouses. There were specific districts reserved for them, such as "La rue des Francs-Bourgeois," "La rue de Truanderie," or "La Cour des Miracles" in Paris. Such actions amounted to a cleaning up of the streets, keeping beggars, cripples, thieves, and unkempt people away so that women of virtue could safely shop in the market or go to church.

For centuries they have fallen victim not only to urbanization but also to disease. Who were the people most affected by the plague? The answer is, the most vulnerable—victims of overcrowding, starvation, and unhygienic conditions. Among them, no attempt was made to care for the sick or to protect the healthy.

Wars as well as great famines took their heaviest toll among the poorest. Think of the Hundred Years War, when communal life in villages and parishes was destroyed and people died of starvation. Think also of France left weakened and drained by the Napoleonic wars, of the deserted countryside, of all the young widows without support, of abandoned children roaming the land. One cannot just say that the people of France had been left prostrate. Who suffered most among those sent to share in the glory of the Napoleonic wars? Who exactly were the three hundred and fifty thousand Bretons who went to fight in the First World War? The whole of Brittany, the whole of France, and the whole of the French people, were not uniformly wiped out. The majority of the victims belonged to the lowest social stratum. For these people, such wars were the final solution, whether planned or not. A factor contributing to their decimation was the practice of giving the rich the opportunity to pay the sons of poor families to go to war in place of their own children. The most underprivileged thus paid for the tribulations and drawbacks of their time. And we often forget that they did not disappear altogether. They returned wounded or maimed, a burden on their families, whom they could no longer support; or, if they disappeared, they left behind a family thrust into destitution.

But the history of France has kept track of such events. You cannot say that these have been erased from our memory?

To keep track is not the same as to write a historical account. A snapshot does not constitute a history. The picture of a soldier coming back on crutches from the Napoleonic wars does not tell us anything about the life of his family or the fate of a disabled father's children. Still less is told of a whole village, a social group, a section of the population deprived of personal possessions and reserves, a majority of whose men have died or are disabled.

Paradoxically, Western Europe, the guardian of Christian civilization, did not bother to tell the story of those who carried on the human condition chosen by Jesus Christ. We may, perhaps, have an idea of the price paid by some for our wars, but we know nothing of the everyday life of the poor or the repercussions on the lives of their children and grandchildren.

Nor do we mention that the same men also paid the price of progress. For they were the ones who bore the cost of the discovery of new continents and the expansion of the merchant marine. They died of scurvy on ships or were taken as galley slaves. Later on, young girls, like the ones found in the pages of Victor Hugo's and Emile Zola's novels, bore the cost of the new consciousness of children's needs that arose at that time. We often have a certain pious attitude toward such characters, but Hugo and Zola revealed the cruel reality of young women who were led to abandon or even kill their children because of their poverty, and who then were prosecuted for murder. Why were they driven to such extremes? Because a more acute awareness of child poverty pointed to the parents as the prime culprits. It still does today, when mothers are compelled to let their children die because of their own state of destitution and abandonment.

All the progress made in the field of health and hygiene has been at the expense of families whose means and knowledge were minimal. We see examples of this every day. In the sixties, when tuberculosis had widely receded, the careful survey of poor districts was stopped. The screening unit van still came, but the medical staff made little effort to ensure that everybody had been examined. However, in the shantytown of Noisy-le-Grand, tuberculosis was still endemic, having affected nearly 80 percent of the families through three generations. When a case arose, the family was all but held responsible, and the local authorities hastened to put children into foster care instead of finding suitable accommodations for the family.

Beatings, shameless exploitation, natural disasters, epidemics—whatever the cause, the most destitute have always been the object of destruction. Whether intentionally or not, such destruction of the poor was often carried out as if for their own good, according to observations made by each new generation: "Instead of concentrating them in the same block of public housing, should we not spread them out? That would be better for them." Or: "They have a lot of children; let's take their children away and prevent them from having more. That would be for their own good." The poorhouse, the orphanage, and the Good Shepherd homes have given way to adoption and educational sponsoring. It does not make the slightest difference; the poor are no more liberated today than they were then. All the member states of the European Community follow the same path: They think they can transplant children from one environment to another, like saplings. The treatment—or, to be more exact, bullying—of the natural parents reflects the lives of the poor, always in the image of the Holy Family fleeing with its threatened child.

According to you, then, we lack a history of the poor; and because our knowledge of their history is so scanty, we are unable to understand our own history.

In order to understand the history of Europe throughout the centuries, we ought to read it through the low ebb the Fourth World represents. We would then gain a better understanding of society's fear of the destitute, its desire to destroy them or, failing that, to "educate" them, to supervise them, to condition and manipulate them. It is no coincidence that they are pushed into temporary provisions, such as "transit" camps and "emergency" accommodations. This is society's way of getting rid of them, of making them disappear. The history of slums is the history of the stable in Bethlehem. It is no coincidence that Joseph was shown to a stable. He was the odd-job man of Nazareth, doing jobs not carried out by a respectable father well-settled on his property or in his village. The innkeeper would not have refused to give accommodation to a worthy craftsman. Nowadays the housing office does not offer a hut, a cellar, or a disused garage to a skilled worker's family.

In Noisy-le-Grand we lived in the greatest poverty, without any means or resources of any kind. When our action gathered momentum, certain public authorities offered us accommodation and grants in the provinces. The families would then be entitled to a decent home, provided they agreed to be sent to some remote country spot. For eight years, families who refused to be deported and who remained near Paris were systematically denied a housing complex. At the time, this fear the authorities had of allowing destitute families to live on the outskirts of Paris seemed to me the consequence of the history of Paris. Did not the men who stormed the Bastille or fought on the barricades of the Commune suddenly appear from the poorest districts of Paris? I was mistaken. On second thought, the rejection of the most destitute—considered to be dangerous, filthy people and used as scapegoats—is an unchanging factor in the history of mankind.

Were the people of the Fourth World revolutionaries? So far, you seem to have implied the opposite.

Fourth World people, although forced to live amid disorder and incoherence, actually like social order; and they like it because they are cautious and realistic. Being constantly despised, excluded, and disappointed, they are well advised to tread carefully. Moreover, people who, throughout their lives, have been victims of disorder and unpredictable events, have a profound desire for harmony. This is probably why the poorest have been exploited for violent actions carried out in the name of order; for example, for breaking a strike or quelling a revolt. On the one hand, it is true they have been called upon in the name of revolution, in which case they rushed to join others in the hope of ensuring the success of a just cause. On the other hand, they have often been manipulated in the name of the established order. Of course, their appearance in mainstream society never lasts very long and, more often than not, they pay a heavy price for it.

This population is sometimes manipulated, sometimes rejected. Between the victims and those responsible for such treatment, what part did the Church play?

If we knew the history of the Fourth World better, we would also be more familiar with the history of the Church. Through all ages, it has reasserted the value of human beings in order to re-introduce them into the community. Are we right in reproaching the Church for not having stopped the exclusion and the rejection of the poor? I do not think so. Within societies where relationships between people have been based on violence for such a long time, where violence was a person's daily bread, how could the Church stop the confinement and the deportation of the poor? Did it have the power to do so? I do not think so. Perhaps we should rephrase the question: could the Church oppose exclusion in any other way than by siding with the excluded, restoring their dignity and reintegrating them?

But was it really present among the poorest?

Always. The Church always stood within the heart of rural pauperism. It was always present near the poor in the cities. We don't know many details because of our insufficient knowledge of the clergy in those areas, who are part of the daily life of the Church. We know hardly anything about those nuns, those priests, and ordinary laypeople who are the hidden life, the unassuming yet strenuous and unrelenting everyday life of the Church. However, it is through their lives and their struggles that the gospel is transmitted and takes root in the hearts and minds of the people.

This hidden Church, day after day, has faithfully carried on with the integration of the poor into the community through education. Even in those periods when civil powers drove the poorest people out of fortified towns, there was, in the cathedral, a priest or sometimes a bishop whose task was to proclaim God's word to the poor. All the works of mercy were dependent on an educational liberation project aimed at both the well-to-do and the poor. The monks who taught peasants to till the land obtained from the lords the means to run their enterprises. Nuns sought the help of the rich to accommodate the poor in hospices, and they taught those rich persons the care of the sick as well as the Good News.

Later on, Vincent de Paul also drew up a real social plan for the poor and for all the faithful. Without the support of his contemporaries, he would not have been able to proclaim, as he did, "The poor, our masters." In actual fact, he summed up and brought to its climax what the Church had already been doing from day to day. In the nineteenth century, the education of the people was still the Church's task.

It seems to me that by these acts of mercy the Church has played into the hands of the rich throughout history.

You may be right in saying the Church has always appeared cautious in its attitude toward major changes affecting the working classes. It has, in fact, always been wary of great upheavals, but not necessarily for the motives usually attributed to it. I must repeat what I said earlier: the Church has a deep-rooted sensitivity to the very poor. The Church is the poor, and it knows they pay a high price for any sudden change. The Church itself pays a high price; many examples of this can be found. The benefits derived from a radical change always go to those who can master it; the weakest suffer its destructive effects. The Church has good reasons to be wary of violent revolutions.

By the way, who are its critics? The affluent and the intellectuals; not the poor. They are the same people who complain that the Fourth World Movement seeks the integration of a so-called "marginal" population into the profit-making consumer society. The accusation would be justified if such integration did not imply a complete change of society.

What does integrating the poor mean? The answer is that teaching the poor and making room for them always involves a radical change in habits and structures.

But since we are dealing with interpretations, we might also criticize the Church for not having been sufficiently innovative in the field of education. In order to equip the poor with a store of general knowledge, it resorted to the means offered by the society of its time: hospices, shelters, and schools. While the Church may have been more creative regarding education, I respect the spirit in which it taught the poor, and I acknowledge the price it paid and is still paying for doing so. Priests and nuns gave what they had; they shared what they knew. Should they have done something else or done it differently? Maybe; but by transmitting an ideal and conveying knowledge, they brought about a reduction in ignorance and armed whole generations of poor people for their struggle. Without the Church, what kind of world would we be living in today?

Certainly the Good Shepherd nuns were no innovators when they gave shelter to young girls who had been caught by the police and made them say the rosary aloud while cleaning windows. But the nuns led a life of poverty and tried to endow these young girls with a trade as well as a faith. I have met a great number of these young women. Although most of them have not followed the moral teaching of the nuns, they show a warm-heartedness, sensitivity, and thoughtfulness toward other people, which are not always found in the young women who are released nowadays from state rehabilitation centers. By welcoming them, not only did the Church try to give them a trade in order to avoid their being dependent on begging and public assistance, but it also took great care in educating their hearts and sharing its spirituality with them.

Would you admit, however, that the Good Shepherd nuns failed to liberate these women?

I never suggested that they liberated them, nor that their practices were the best for their time. But I maintain that the Church did not send the poor into the world without arming them to deal with the difficulties of life. Think of Father Brottier, the founder of "Les Orphelins d'Auteuil,"[10] of the numerous congregations created after the fall of the First Empire, and of the laypeople in countless numbers who have devoted themselves to the underprivileged throughout the ages. They all had a comprehensive plan, that is, to build an ideal and a trade. Maybe striving toward an ideal of independence for the young is more revolutionary than it seemed at the time.

More fundamentally, the Church always seeks to protect the poorest, especially from bogus types of liberation. As much as the poor themselves, it has good reason to be wary of any kind of liberation; not that it or they reject the idea, but it must lead to real and total liberation for the lame, the crippled, the blind; it must embrace the leper and put the poorest first. True liberation will give those who are rejected the means to be free without becoming, in turn, the oppressors.

The Church—through its prudent and reserved attitude as much as through its progressive action—maintains, in the collective memory of humankind, the refusal to accept injustice and destitution. All this it did with much selflessness. Whatever one may say, without the Church we would not have the same sense of liberty, justice, and truth. Such an interpretation of the facts is, no doubt, a personal one, but I maintain it. In any case, we are dealing with interpretations that historians are hardly inclined to verify.

Would you apply this last comment to the recent historians? Are we not witnessing a new understanding of the history of the poor?

Recent historians touch on the history of the poorest and, consequently, on the history of the Church. But to go further into that history would necessitate a great sensitivity and knowledge of destitution today in order to be able to recognize the signs of destitution in the past. The history of pilgrimages comes to mind; it suggests that the wandering poor formed the backdrop—poor people condemned to go on pilgrimage for petty thefts. Persons who are aware of extreme poverty notice such signs. Other authors write about pilgrimages without even being aware they have come close to the life of the poorest.

You agree that historians are not unaware of the history of the poor in the nineteenth century. We learn their history in our earliest years at school.

I am not at all certain of this. As far as the plight of the poorest is concerned, we are content, at best, with a very vague knowledge. Who can tell, with precision, what the turning point of their destiny was? Who were their witnesses?

The prominent actors in the history of humanity take an interest in the most destitute only after the event, after situations have been created. But previously they ignored those persons they deemed useless: "We shall deal with them later on." The same thing happens when changes are made in the name of the poor. At the beginning of the twentieth century, Lenin wanted to better the situation of the people by committing himself to the cause of the peasants and then to the cause of the workers. Others had tried before him. But misunderstandings arise and good intentions are quickly eroded whenever it is a question of siding with a very poor population whose experience of life is unknown to us. Educated people are carried away by their own ideas and always end up doing the thinking for others. This is what happened to Lenin and his circle of intellectuals.

Perhaps it is not for us Christians to criticize him for that, but we must be more severe with ourselves. We have the example of Christ, who is probably the only one who saw the liberation of the poorest through to the end, with them. Believers do not always imitate him, even today. They, too, fall into the trap of efficiency and haste. This is true of most of the movements in which believers are involved. They undoubtedly mean no harm to the underprivileged, but they believe they have no time for them. They regard the poor as a burden interfering with neat analyses. We can understand this attitude coming from Marxists, experts in the doctrine of exploitation, but not coming from Christians, who have always been taught about rejection and exclusion. Christians ought to question the past and the present in a different way. For if they do not, they allow a historical misconception to prevail—that the situation of the underprivileged and that of the workers is one and the same. This would be true if the two groups concerned had shared the same history, from the nineteenth century onwards, more closely. That was not the case; but because we persist in ignoring this fact, we cannot understand what is happening to the poorest nowadays. As far as Christians are concerned, such ignorance is hardly admissible. We ought to be more eager to recognize the Lord's face in every age.

To your mind, searching for Jesus Christ, searching for historical truth, and searching for the poorest in our day are one and the same.

I cannot see things otherwise; moreover, I believe that the liberation of the poorest worldwide demands an understanding of their history. At least as regards the West, only through history can we explain the presence at our door of those men and women who constantly face the threat of unemployment, who are always potentially, if not chronically, unemployed.

You asked me a question about the transmission of misery, and I told you it was handed down from generation to generation through common experiences of life. Perhaps the worst experiences are those encountered on the job. For what makes the poorest people most ashamed is that they are not considered workers like any other; they are always treated as inferiors, even in the workplace. This sense of inferiority gives rise to the shame they feel everywhere—with their wives and children, at the town hall, at school, at the hospital, and even when they go shopping. Worse than their sense of inferiority when facing the boss is their lack of self-esteem when with their fellow workers, who are always better qualified and have more skill and confidence than they. Such is the unbearable burden of the underprivileged, a burden that weighs heavily on those who live in low-income neighborhoods.

In the sixties, the Fourth World Movement sought to restore the families' pride in being the sub-proletariat. It was not enough to use the term "Fourth World." We had to proclaim their rightful place among today's working people. In 1787, Dufourny de Villiers referred to this group as the "Fourth Order." Karl Marx described the same workers—or their descendants—as the "Lumpenproletariat."

Do you mean to say that the same families are reproduced generation after generation?

Their history is more complex; but, here again, we do not get much help from the historians. We have carried out our own extensive research with families in deprived areas, especially with the most disadvantaged among them. We have traced family trees and reconstituted thousands of family histories. We have thus been able, together, to discover information about the marriages, the relationships, and the descendants. Throughout the history of these families, we found poverty, hunger, obscure or shameful jobs, vagrancy, frequent rejection from parishes, dependence on charity, and finally, ignorance, since destitution and illiteracy always go hand in hand.

Could not the same be said of many working-class families now well integrated?

Probably, but I am not certain. Within the working masses of the nineteenth century there were, despite everything, hierarchies and different kinds of jobs and workers. On the one hand, there were very poor, ignorant people doing the roughest jobs; on the other hand, there were those for whom life was not so wretched; these two groups did not see much of each other. Whose descendants are today's poor?

One thing is certain: The Fourth World families whose history we have been able to reconstitute are descendants, for the most part, of the poorest people. From my own experience, I can add that it takes time to turn a person into someone who is "below the working class." People do not easily let themselves be pushed down like that. I saw that in my own family and in many others.

In my family, would it have been possible for us to sink to such depths? We experienced lack of money and food, a hovel with no light, and handouts and humiliations. We had to work for money at a very early age; every night, including weekends, we fitted pads of Zig-Zag cigarette papers into cardboard packets. In our family, the children entered the worker's life through subcontracting. Every Thursday, we took our boxes to the factory to earn a few pennies. Every evening, after school, we had to complete a box, as well as on Thursday morning before going to the church youth club or out to play.

It is probably thanks to my mother's strength of character that we were able to pull through. She had inherited this from her Spanish-Catholic upbringing. She defended us. She fought tooth and nail because she had not been brought up in poverty herself in her hometown of Madrid. In order not to rely on begging, she walked all the way to the upper part of the town of Angers to do several hours of housework. By making her own children work for the Zig-Zag company, my mother was refusing to beg. Charity was all around us but we withstood it, though we did not succeed entirely in our attempt. My older brother and I were altar boys and we went to serve Mass every morning at the Good Shepherd Convent. We earned only a few pennies, but we were also given food, a share in the meals the Madeleine Sisters had. So, from the age of four and a half to fourteen, I was able to bring food home to my mother. The clothes I was wearing were also given to me. But, as far as my mother was concerned, dignity was paramount and depended on the manner in which things were given to us. She did not accept just any old kind of clothing and never allowed herself to be treated without respect. She cried over affronts shown her, but I also saw her ostensibly refuse to greet people who had shown a lack of consideration the week before.

I have often witnessed a similar resistance to destitution in the Fourth World. Of course we find the most impoverished people there, whose plight dates back, as we have seen, to the eighteenth century, even the seventeenth century. These people have nothing to hold on to in their struggle for survival. But, others have only recently been pushed down to the bottom rung of the social ladder. Among the thousands of families known by Fourth World Movement teams, we do not see any sudden change. Only rarely do people fall from a very high position. Those who come to live in sub-standard dwellings are people who have known very precarious living standards before. The famous doctor turned tramp or the well-integrated working-class family that suddenly falls victim to extreme poverty seem rather to belong to the realm of legend. Such stories ignore people's resilience (and that, too, is applicable to migrant workers) and also denote a kind of scornful attitude toward our fellow citizens stranded at the bottom of the social ladder. They overlook all the sufferings the very poor have been through before they got into this plight, all their attempts to resist the misfortune of exclusion, all their repeated efforts every minute to get out of it.

You think, therefore, that it is from the lowest strata of the working class that a person is pushed into the Fourth World. But what about the exodus from the countryside to the cities? In the sixties, this was considered one of the causes of marginalization.

Migration within a society is part of the fate of the most destitute. I have already mentioned the way in which they are hounded or arbitrarily displaced. Even if this were not so, many would be on the roads in search of a better life. Many among the very poor families living in Paris have come from the provinces. Trying to find out their geographical places of origin did not add much to our knowledge. It seems more important to know what their jobs were, the work and the living conditions of their parents, whether they lived in an urban setting or a rural one. We find that they were always very poor, if not outright destitute.

Let me give you the example of a farm worker from Brittany. Before the war, his father was a logger, a poor man's job in his region. This father, who died before reaching the age of fifty, had taught the son to wield an axe. This son, left without a secure job, had to support his brothers and sisters. Later on, he married a young woman from the same village and from a poor family, too.

We found the names of these two families in parish registers, among those who had received aid during the worst winter months. Who were these newlyweds: poor or even destitute people? Possibly, but at least they lived in a village where they were known and received support. One day they left the village because they wanted to live independent lives. Some years later they ended up in a housing project in the Paris area, where they lived with their children in utter destitution. When I saw their home, I often thought of my own mother's unremitting efforts. For, in the first of their two rooms, there was a cupboard with neatly arranged linen. This cupboard was a sure sign of their resistance. Throughout the years I knew this family, through all the humiliations and setbacks they experienced, the linen cupboard remained there. The man had long since become unemployed, and the children had been put into foster care by the social services. The mother had finally given up and taken to drink. But the traditional Breton linen cupboard was still in its place, a last gesture of defiance against misery.

I could give you many similar examples. Contrary to what people like to say, I do not think drinking is the cause of the poor's misery. It is simply that people reach such a degree of inferiority that they can no longer remain friendly with their neighbors. Their lives are so fraught with problems that they can no longer see what they might have in common with a society that ignores them. But this happens to them almost imperceptibly, like a slow descent, not a sudden fall. And in the course of this gradual decline, at least for the first generation, the family takes its roots with them. They keep what they can of their culture, of their original habits and manners. But they are like plants transplanted from a field into pots. When the original soil is exhausted, the plants die. In the Fourth World, the soil is no longer nourished or renewed.

At this lowest level, we find an underprivileged people that welcomes but does not nurture. At least they are there. They make no demands on you, nor do they bring you anything. Because this underprivileged population exists, poor working-class families can be drawn into it. But I must repeat: I have never known formerly affluent families to fall into a state of severe poverty by accident. Once more, we are led to acknowledge that the underprivileged constitute a people because they have had similar experiences and life stories. This means similar work patterns: temporary jobs, underemployment, and unemployment. Such conditions create a people who react to the outside world with a common sensitivity. They all suffer in the realization that they are the shameful face of the working class. Kinship, environment, and dependence on the same social services contribute to keeping them in a specific social group.

Have changes in the rural world and urbanization contributed to the increase in the number of underprivileged families?

They have brought to light a previously hidden poverty. It already existed but was not as visible as it is today. Although these changes have made the condition of the poorest more distressing, they do not seem to have led a great number of new families into deep poverty. In fact, the opposite opinion was expressed in the sixties and seventies, when it was thought that maladjustment and exclusion were a widespread threat. This is not what I observed in the poorest housing projects of France or in neighboring countries.

On the other hand, since the start of the recession, an increased number of new poverty-stricken families have arrived. They are often sent to housing projects by social services that no longer know how to meet their needs. I would not say that unemployment necessarily leads to destitution, but I would like to offer a specific observation. The economic crisis has more disastrous consequences among workers who are already underprivileged than among other categories of workers, although the latter risk falling into the abyss if their unemployment persists. In any event, the humiliation that layoffs inflict on unskilled workers undermines their physical and moral stamina, especially when the family has no social or cultural assets or financial resources.

The civic and religious communities should try to protect these families in particular. But long-term unemployment at the lowest rungs of the social ladder is not a widely known fact—its victims do not arouse comment; when they sink lower, they meet with widespread indifference.

I am surprised not to hear you mention migrant workers. Public opinion is very concerned with them. Don't they belong to the Fourth World, too?

We must refuse to group them that way, out of respect, for the majority of them are not part of the Fourth World. Not that their material and social condition is better, but at least they have a recognized identity, and their situation can be explained and justified. If they are unemployed, we know why. It is not their own fault, but the consequence of the economic circumstances of the moment or of the job market. Unemployment among French underprivileged workers, who were already underemployed or out of work before the crisis, cannot be so easily explained. People will say of them: "He's unstable. He's always been so." "He is looking for work but prays to God that he won't find any."

A moment ago, you emphasized the need to recognize the underprivileged as having the status of workers. Yet you speak mainly of underemployment and unemployment.

The reason for this emphasis is that when we examine the situation very closely, we realize that the underprivileged have had a long history of work, and that the tasks they carry out are more often than not the most humble, arduous, and disheartening ones. A great number of men in the Fourth World are given jobs on the fringe of public works and the contracting business; for instance, they work as ditchdiggers, masons' aids, sweepers, demolition workers, hired men of all kinds. Others work in the most marginal small firms and in industrial sectors that are in difficulty, such as the skin and leather trade, foodstuffs, the metallurgical industry, furniture manufacturing, and the chemical and textile industries. A last group falls back on agriculture and unskilled jobs on the outer edges of industry: they help unload trucks, move furniture, and clean workplaces, sewers, and garbage trucks, often at night. They are undertakers' assistants, do the most repugnant jobs in hospitals, and clean railroad cars and toilets in stations at night. They assemble market stalls, sweep refuse, clean ship holds in the merchant marine, deliver messages, carry advertisement boards, shine shoes, wash dishes, peel vegetables in restaurants, distribute leaflets, and clean windows.

But enumerating the jobs done by the underprivileged in this way is not enough. In order to have a true idea of the lot of these workers, we must bear in mind the usual pattern of their working lives. We then discover situations in which, very often and for generations, job follows job, periods of inactivity grow longer as workers get older, and chances of promotion fade as a worker's performance diminishes due to premature aging and declining health. Another feature of these working lives is that the most arduous jobs are carried out without work contracts; that is to say, without any reference to work regulations. Consequently, employers take almost no interest in this work force for which they have no legal responsibility.

6.

Sub-Proletarian Workers, the Suffering Face of the Working World

Gilles Anouil: In fact, the condition of the most disadvantaged is a situation that affects life in general. You often speak of a condition that has to be approached as a whole; yet you say it is the employment situation that determines all other aspects of Fourth World life. What, therefore, is the role of trade unions?

Father Joseph Wresinski: I have never met any workers, whether union members or not, who do not feel some empathy for the most disadvantaged among their coworkers. You need only talk to a few of them to realize they all come from families who had some firsthand experience with poverty. The most disadvantaged workers are part of the working world, and there was a time, not so long ago, when experiences of life were not all that different from each other. People will say to you, "Now that I think of it, my grandfather's brother was also a farm worker; my father said he had a hard life because he had seven children and jobs were getting scarce."

Workers' movements probably carry this same sensitivity within them.

Deep down, they do not accept the idea of not being close to all the workers and of not struggling for everyone. But you have to put yourself in the shoes of those activist organizations, which are always hard at it, always on the alert, even when conditions get better. They have to constantly defend what has been won; to acquire, or rather, to grab hold, of new rights for the workers, to concentrate on what is currently happening, to face the immediate challenge and to be on the defensive. All this creates a mindset for struggle, a need to choose priorities so as to be efficient, all the while remaining united and advancing in very close ranks.

With this in mind, in our modern society, can we concentrate fully on those "inefficient" people who make life so difficult? At best, the active trade unionists feel embarrassed by, and are suspicious of, those who remind them that not all workers are helped by their union, that the poorest are being left behind. Pointing this out causes a division within the working class. I myself have been reproached on this issue, and I can understand their anxiety. The motivation of trade unionists to fight on behalf of everyone cannot be questioned. The fact that they haven't succeeded must not be attributed to workers' movements. Once again, a whole society, a whole national and even international community, is responsible.

Do active members of the large trade union organizations show their concern for the most disadvantaged workers?

I meet their representatives at the Economic and Social Council, where my concerns do not seem unfamiliar to them. But I was also a grass-roots activist when I was a young worker. I think I can understand the difficulties they are having at that level of the work force. In their workplaces, employees are sincere in that they struggle on behalf of everyone. "All the workers," in their daily struggle, means "all fellow workers in the shop," "all fellows in the factory," "all the skilled workers." But not everyone is a skilled worker; there are areas of activity that the unions do not reach; there are occupations that are incorrectly categorized in the job market analyses. That whole reality is beyond them. To be an active trade unionist already requires a great deal of energy, time, and courage. I am not sure they can see beyond their workplace in order to see those irregular, seasonal, or even temporary workers who are the most disadvantaged.

Let me give you an example. I am thinking of an active member of a railroad union whom I knew when I was in Tergnier. He and his wife devoted all their lives and leisure time to the trade union struggle to the point of neglecting their garden. He was held in great respect at his workplace, but in his small, closely-knit neighborhood, it was another matter. The neighbors were very critical of them for neglecting their garden, as he was always at meetings and congresses. Can you imagine that this man could possibly listen when I came to talk to him about "La Pomme Rouge" or about the Cité de Beautor?[11] The same applied to his coworkers. Many of them would not give up work in their garden to attend a meeting. But they also had constant worries regarding their families, their children, and their health.

But all members are not equally overwhelmed by work in the unions. Some are relatively at ease.

An activist is never at ease. Everything conspires to confine workers' unions to the factory, to lock them in at the workplace. As soon as they go beyond the problems of their factory, they are accused of political action. They are confined to the factory in the same way as the priest used to be confined to the sacristy and the Pope to the church. This is nonsense; but for politicians, it is a way of getting rid of those who are seen as troublesome. You must admit that, under these conditions, it is difficult for trade unions to defend workers who are rejected from organized sectors of economic activity.

If I understand rightly, trade unions do not include the most disadvantaged workers; but this is an unintended omission.

Perhaps we could say it results from ignorance. The most disadvantaged, as we said earlier, appear as strangers to the world that surrounds them. This also applies to the world of work. Workers may have a lingering memory of the realities of extreme poverty, but it is quite a different matter to meet those who are unqualified, right on the building site or in the factory yard. The less skilled such people are, the more they pretend to know things. What are others to make of it? Furthermore, unskilled workers are often not punctual in coming to work. Fellow workers do not accept that some people arrive late; it undermines the workers' conscience. The boss is allowed to miss work, but the work mates are not. Recently one of the Fourth World volunteers, working on an assembly line, attempted to defend those workers. As a result he alienated all the others. I also remember some women from a very poor housing project who were hired to clean railroad cars. They also had, nearby, a full-time volunteer from the Movement. He was never able to defend their interests.

Generally speaking, Fourth World workers behave as people who are uprooted from the world of work. They have never been fully part of it or, if they have, it was under conditions that did not allow them to completely adopt the routines of the other workers, such as their ways of talking or putting tools away. Furthermore, they might seek an agreement directly with the boss when they should have gone through a delegate. They do not have the knack of being workers, nor have they any means of learning it.

In fact, they entered the world of work through the wrong door, the door of child labor. I took that same door, as I told you before, when packing the Zig-Zag cigarette papers. I worked every day, even Sundays. Subcontracted work or working as a child does not give a person the taste for work or teach the spirit of the workers' struggles. Yet there are still many children who go to school half asleep because they rose too early. They have already done hours of work to help their father or mother. They are prematurely useful to their family. When the time comes to seek a real job, they no longer have the health or the taste for it; that is, assuming there is even a job available for them.

The fact that they work early in life does not prepare them for future jobs, then? The opposite was said in previous generations.

Nothing could be further from the truth nowadays. In the past, workers' children or farm children were being prepared for their future lives because they were involved in jobs with adults; they learned the art of working from them. Nowadays, what Fourth World children do has nothing to do with their future job situation. Their experience is almost an anti-training. The training for social and professional life happens at school. That is where children of workers get trained. In school they not only receive intellectual knowledge, but they also gain social experience. In the past, disadvantaged young people could gain that experience by being an apprentice with a local baker or butcher. Nowadays, school is their only opportunity.

When they are deprived of training, are young people and adults doomed to be unemployed?

The underprivileged worker has been under-employed or unemployed—with or without a reprieve—since an early age. Nowadays it is often not even a question of long-term unemployment. Young people are faced with unemployment for life without ever having worked.

For example, the Research Institute of the Fourth World Movement did an analysis based on the last forty years in France, which shows that the rate of unemployment for unskilled workers was nearly always twice the national average. For underprivileged workers, the rate was nearly twice the total for unskilled workers.

In the period from 1954 to 1964, the unemployment rate was between 0.5 percent and 1.9 percent. Unskilled workers formed 50 percent of the total number of unemployed, whereas they formed only 13 percent of the working population. For this period there are no statistics for the underprivileged.

In 1968 the rate of unemployment was an average of 2.1 percent; for unskilled workers it was 5.4 percent. But in a housing project for the underprivileged in France, the rate was 9.2 percent at that time.

In 1979 the rate of unemployment was an average of 7.6 percent, and for unskilled workers it was 13.0 percent. Whereas, in May 1981, the unemployment rate among the underprivileged was 31.8 percent. In 1981 the unemployment rate for Fourth World young people in four French towns reached a level of 44.3 percent.

We are aware, however, of the unequal way in which unemployment affects workers in France. In the Paris area, there was a specific campaign recently started to help the long-term unemployed.

That's true, but there is a double pitfall to this. First of all, the long-term unemployed fall into quite a vast and diverse category. This gives potential employers a wide choice among job seekers, allowing them to turn first to those persons who are easiest to reach. We often hear talk of reaching "women," "young people," "the over-fifties," "the unemployed." Unless the special terms "the less qualified," "the less productive," or "the less resilient" are added, such people will not be targeted. And if there is no special effort made, they will not be reached.

Not only will they not be reached, but no one will even know they have been excluded. In France, our inability to evaluate the results of our struggles plays against the poor. Who benefits from what, exactly? It is not a matter of knowing how many citizens benefit from a measure or an organization, but rather who these citizens are. This question is asked regularly in the Scandinavian and Benelux countries, in Great Britain and in the United States. But in France we are doctrinaire; we think that if our reasoning is good and just, we are supposed to have good and just results. We are also impatient people. We don't let measures take root and bear fruit. I fear this may be the case with the campaign against long-term unemployment. We may know, one day, how many workers have benefited, but we won't know who they are.

Does this evaluation problem also affect workers' movements?

The unions do not divulge all their evaluations. But I notice that, in their publications, membership among the least qualified and those least integrated into the job market is not particularly stressed. The participation of the most disadvantaged workers is not presented as a major objective. Workers' demands do not always encompass the needs of men and women who are engaged in tasks that are without prestige, poorly paid, and liable to disappear with any future modernization. Demands for better pay do not necessarily concern these employment sectors. Most of the rights of employed people are, moreover, coupled with minimum obligations that cannot be honored by those who have the worst jobs. For instance, one has to work several months without interruption in order to be eligible for an allowance or a pension. With one thing leading to another, we have allowed ourselves to structure the world of work in a way that is unfavorable and even extremely unfair to people of the Fourth World. This imperceptible but constant shift has evidently not been a deliberate choice on the part of trade unions. But how can we put things right in a time of crisis? We should have been more careful at the start. Priority for the poorest must be there from the beginning; it is never gained along the way.

The reduction in working hours, self-management, and the transformation of work brought about by the production line—have none of these achievements benefited the poorest?

The unfavorable chain of events has already gone a long way. How can you stem the flow? You mention improved working conditions; these affect workers who are actually employed. And as a consequence, those who do not have a lively and creative spirit, or a precise and rapid way of working, will be less and less likely to be employed. Fourth World workers suffer from rheumatism because of their living conditions. They have constant headaches and stomachaches. Their health is generally poor, and they cannot do simple movements with precision. Nor can they keep up with a rhythm of work. If you watch these men and women work, you will understand that they are not going to benefit from the advantages you mention. The working world will benefit insofar as it has inherited a long history of work well done and a patient initiation to occupations that are more and more sophisticated.

You forget vocational training and, even before that, school education. Can't everything change—at least for the young at the bottom of the social ladder?

Everything can change indeed, but it requires major efforts and determination. At the present time, the poorest children are not on the road to participating in the economic life of the future. We see an increasing number of them at ever-younger ages being sent to special education programs. These are "special" only in that they expect nothing from the child. The children feel inferior to other children their age, and they suffer from this to the point of forever losing their taste for learning. The school not only subtly robs them of an education, but it also deprives them, as I said before, of a vital social experience. They do not learn what a community could be. They are not really part of the school. Even their mealtimes are different from those in "normal" classes.

As for vocational training, the European Community Social Fund has for many years been financing programs that are supposedly pilot programs for young people without qualifications or adequate schooling. We have studied these programs one by one. None of them takes into account a young person who has not succeeded in at least primary education; yet children who live in substandard housing, old trucks, shacks, and discarded railroad cars have no possibility of achieving primary education, or even the chance to properly learn how to read and write. It is always the same problem. We don't systematically ask ourselves the question: Do our efforts really include everyone? Do we look for those who cannot follow? Who are they? Where are they?

You reproach your contemporaries, who live in constant questioning, for not asking the right questions.

Constant questioning is unavoidable if we want to continue to consider ourselves inheritors of a civilization that has given birth to the idea of human rights. Our civilization has also previously given birth to the idea of the priority of the poorest. In any case, Jesus Christ and the Church ask us to question ourselves ceaselessly: Where is the Lord?

In your opinion, is he in the Fourth World?

We cannot identify the Lord in this way; we have to meet Jesus Christ. It is not an intellectual endeavor or a personal opinion, but an experience. The Lord is perhaps not where we would like to find him. Normally he leads us rather to where we don't wish to go. He spent his life being something else and being somewhere else, not being what his contemporaries wanted him to be. Jesus cannot be manipulated. That is why I am hesitant when some young people want to make Jesus Christ the hero of their revolutions. I am hesitant when certain activists in the workers' movement say that Jesus is necessarily one of them. I recently heard the homily of a pastor who saw Christ as an ecologist, protesting against the irresponsible use of energy. I would be reassured if they told me: That's where I personally met him. That would be irrefutable, since the Lord appears to each one of us in the way he deems right.

It is another thing to go and look for him. Then it is to our advantage to use the compass given us by the gospel. This will not lead us to one political camp rather than another, to one social class rather than another. Rather, it leads us always toward something beyond, toward something outside the town, toward hidden paths where no one wants to go. When I said, "Where is the Lord?" I mean, "Where are we going to find him?" Perhaps he will escape us. It is our mission, however, to evaluate all our policies and every effort according to the question: Have we really gone as far as we could, right to the most excluded, thus being as sure as we can that we have Christ with us constantly?

Are these opportunities offered to us in the Fourth World?

For me, the Lord is there as if in passing, if I may say so. Tomorrow I shall have to look for him further away. Perhaps I shall have to look for him among those workers who are despised by their neighbors and whom I met in one of the most dreadful shantytowns on the West African coast. Already Jesus is waiting for us elsewhere, perhaps in those Latin American villages where we have trouble identifying the inhabitants. They have been driven to such destitution that they can no longer claim any culture or call themselves native Americans. That is one place the Movement volunteers have chosen to be in recent years in their search for the poorest.

In the meantime, how can we help believing we saw the Lord in the man who was on his way back to his neighborhood in the north, in Rheims or in

Caen, profoundly hurt because he was fired once again? He was expecting to lose his job because he had a temporary position pushing small trucks loaded with packages. Throughout his six weeks of employment, he felt, without really admitting it to himself, that he was a stranger in the place. He knew he was not one of the "real workers." But at least he was able to walk around the housing project with his head held high. His wife would tell anyone who cared to hear, "My husband has a job!" Now he has been fired again, with no hope of finding anything for a long time. In the project, the previously envious people now chuckle: "That will pull her down a peg or two, that woman. Why did she have to boast like that?"

The debts of this man do not wait for unemployment in order to accumulate; they were there long before. But that is not the worst. The worst pain is to come home like that, humiliated as always. The man has been fired, without a protest from anyone. He is fully aware that things like this do not happen to skilled workers. He has even seen a work stoppage for the benefit of skilled workers who were threatened with layoffs. As for him, nobody protests when he leaves. He is what he has always been: an inferior person, a man who does not count in the eyes of his fellow workers. He does not count in his housing project, either. His neighbors are rivals who covet his job. He will not find solidarity there. In the evening, when I go and see him, he does not say anything. His wife is crying. Both the anguish of finding herself thrown out on to the streets—as has often happened before, since her childhood—and the fear of losing custody of her children, have returned to the household.

I can't help feeling the presence of that carpenter, Joseph, when I am in these housing projects. He was a worker, fleeing into a foreign land where he was forbidden to cultivate the soil. What could he do? He could only break stones, cart the soil, always fighting for survival. We are told that in Nazareth he was in reality a laborer. What was a laborer to do in a community so poor that nothing positive was expected of it? What was a carpenter to do in a village where all the men knew how to work with wood for domestic purposes? What tasks were left to the carpenter, in a rural community where woodworking as a noble trade fell to the head of a family? When I think of Joseph's living conditions and those of the shepherds, I ask myself whether we fail to assess the role of the poorest, even in the gospel. Do we see who they are?

I would like to come back again to trade unionism. Since you mention the gospels...do you think that even workers' organizations of Christian inspiration are not defending the poorest?

They certainly defend the poorest, and I have told you I think all worker movements are attempting to do this. The question, however, remains the same: Who, in their eyes, are the poorest? Do they see those whom we see?

Let me tell you about something that happened to me when I was a deacon. I was working for a paint manufacturing company, grinding powder in vats in the basement. The people who worked there were unknown to the other workers. We all belonged to the "underclass," working together, and no one came to propose that we join a union. No one came to see us or inquired about our working conditions. Even in the dining hall we remained together.

One day, people in the company found out I was going to leave because, in fact, I was a deacon and I had to go back to the seminary. Word spread, and on the day of my departure, an elderly worker who was sticking labels onto cans in the factory yard came toward me. He said, "They told me that you're a deacon and that you're leaving. Why didn't you tell me you were a deacon?" Then he took out a handful of application forms for membership in the CFTC (the Christian workers' union). He added, "You should have told me. I would have given you some for the guys down below."

That is where the division lies: a unionized worker cannot imagine speaking directly to the "guys down below." Those guys, in his mind, could not be unionized unless they had a sponsor. In the factory, those working with the vats in the basement were not seen the same as the other workers. I think that, in fact, trade unionists do not know what to do with underprivileged workers. They believe these men and women have given up and dropped out. Therein lies a big misunderstanding that separates people from one another. However, underprivileged workers have only one desire: to be recognized as workers, not only to be at the same level as others, but to be fully integrated with them. The underprivileged see workers as belonging to a world of security and respectability, in which they are represented and defended. In all this, it is the "collective" worthiness that they need the most and that is the most valuable to them, because they want to be recognized as people who belong.

For its part, organized labor may not recognize this deep desire of the underprivileged to be part of the working world's struggles, because labor has inherited soundness and nobility in what Marx termed "the hard and fortifying school of work." It has a history of struggle, endurance, and injustice borne and rejected with honor. Not everyone took an active part in the struggles, but everyone benefits from them. Everyone can say, "Here is the fruit of our struggles. It is our right." This is how they talk among themselves, in their families or among workers in the dining hall. Underprivileged workers do not have this heritage; they have neither its language nor its mentality. Their own history has gone off track, and today they feel they deserve nothing and have no rights. At the agency, they beg for temporary work and sometimes even offer to give money on the side to get a job. Their ancestors used to go to the towns on Saint Martin's day to sell themselves to a farmer for one year. Currently they go to a temporary job agency to sell themselves for three weeks. And, as they are looking for unskilled labor, they are regarded in the same way as their great-grandfathers were: "That guy doesn't look very strong. Will he be up to it?" It is a deep humiliation when they are deemed unfit; then they are forced to let social workers into their homes, and they are afraid of them; whereas a worker's household, which respects itself, hardly knows the social workers and would not let them interfere in family affairs.

We must understand the difference between a group of people who know they have rights even if these are not respected, and those for whom no right is ever ensured, where work is never secure and nearly always temporary. Insecurity itself is hard enough to bear. These differences manifest themselves in vocabulary, in attitudes, and even in the way people walk. It is extremely painful to be different from and feel inferior to others. It is an experience of life that is constantly degrading, with no end in sight.

To sum up, is it the fact of not being involved in workers' struggles that perpetuates the condition of the underprivileged?

Yes, that's right; and I am sure the underprivileged will get out of their condition if they are recognized by the working world. That's where the key to their liberation lies, and it is possible to achieve. I have known many active union members at the grass-roots level. They are of a certain caliber, and with them it should be possible to make progress. They are usually quite different from politicians. They have their feet firmly on the ground and they have the necessary sensitivity. I have never understood why organizations of Christian inspiration don't go ahead and start a relentless fight against destitution.

Can they do this without enrolling underprivileged workers? Otherwise, how will they bridge the gap that separates them? The most disadvantaged will not come of their own accord because they haven't got the union spirit.

It is readily said that the poorest have no political sense and that they are incapable of understanding institutions. This is said throughout the world. Rather, I believe that underprivileged workers are realists. By their attitude, they give us an important lesson.

For, what is a structure? In everyday life, it means a counter, a room, or a meeting. If you are forced to go there as a beggar who has no rights to assert, if you cannot master the language and you feel awkward, how can you help feeling totally ill at ease? Under these conditions, the successful outcome of the steps you take will depend on the people who welcome you. Are they haughty, or friendly and understanding? Will they reproach you or help you? For underprivileged families, that is the reality of a structure. They have every reason to worry about people rather than rules. All the more so because the families nearly always ask for things that the people behind the desk are in a perfectly good position to let them have. It is not because the coffers are empty that an official at the town hall does not approve a request for help. At the Family Allowance Office, it is possible to approve an advance on payments that were interrupted because a family moved. A boss could grant one day's leave because an employee's wife is ill and there is no one to drive her to the hospital, to go shopping, or to prepare meals for the children.

On the surface, daily life in the Fourth World is very much at the mercy of such trivial things. All that is required is a nice gesture, a bit of kindness. That is where the tragedy of families lies—in always having to count on the goodwill of others; that is all that is left when there are no unconditional rights to housing, family allowances, unemployment benefits, or whatever the household needs.

Is it a lack of a sense of structures, or is it just reality? I am not saying underprivileged workers understand the complexities of trade unions or other structures, which they don't know how to use and constantly fear. For instance, they may confront a boss or a section head directly, when the appropriate route is via a personnel delegate. They will say that, in any case, they can't see the difference: "Those people are on the side of the boss... at the wrong end of the line... It's better to talk to God than to the saints."

Many are astonished at this tendency to go directly to people in the highest position while ignoring intermediate structures. Disadvantaged families, if they know how to write, send their requests directly to the President. I do admit that this shows a certain ignorance of political matters. But, in fact, by corresponding with the head of state, they give us a lesson on the reliability of the structures. Most of the time they need a recourse: Perhaps an apartment has been refused them, or a request for a disabled person's allowance has been lying round the office for eighteen months because the applicant hasn't worked long enough to receive it as a right. They address themselves to a person of stature, to someone wrapped in the myth of power. Would they do this if their requests were accepted at lower levels in the hierarchy? They say, "We know who he is; he will answer us."

Isn't this a situation in which people who are weak are looking for a sort of protective paternalism?

That is said about them, but it is quite inaccurate. It is easy to find superficial and denigrating explanations of why the poorest act the way they do. When the poor wrote to de Gaulle, during the time of the large shantytowns, they were thinking, "We are suffering an injustice, we need a recourse." And according to the Constitution, they were perfectly right. Heads of state have to make sure that the Constitution is applied with regard to human rights. They must place themselves above political parties. That is precisely the sort of essential recourse for the Fourth World, since all their basic rights are systematically infringed upon. You can see that the very poor do exactly the same in the Netherlands or in Belgium. They write to the Queen.

Does this produce the desired results?

It often answers immediate requests by providing interim help or housing. But that is not the point. The main thing is that the underprivileged give us a lesson in political science: Our democratic structures do not ensure human rights for everyone. For the most disadvantaged, not only do they not ensure representation, but they also do not provide any form of recourse. "I am not asking the President for the moon. I am only asking to get back my family allowance," a father told me. He was not asking for a change in society, and in that he was right. Our democratic structures, while allowing the head of state to attend to the application of the Constitution, do not provide him with the means to change these structures. Rather, to effect change, the poorest need to go through the representation process in parliament. And underprivileged families know full well that there is no mention of them in the Chamber of Deputies.

The history of our democracies proves the workers of the Fourth World right. Neither systems nor doctrines come anywhere near eradicating injustice. With each new generation, everything depends on people. The poorest tell us this, not because they are uncultured but because of the sensitivity to realities that they have acquired through the ages. By transmitting a concrete experience from parents to children, a whole population group also transmits a very special sense of the importance of the individual person.

I detected this same sensitivity recently at a meeting with about fifty very poor families in London. A lawyer had come to talk to them about foster care for children. As long as they spoke of their own experiences—the anguish and the frustration of parents and children—the discussion was warm and lively. When the lawyer began to propose an organized and programmed defense scheme, everyone became quiet.

But then what should we do? What can the unions do? Even Marx complained about the proletariat as having little inclination to organize itself and become a force. The conclusion he drew was that the proletariat had no fighting spirit and that it needed someone to combat in its place.

That is a hasty conclusion. You can't judge the fighting spirit or the aspirations of people by how quickly they organize themselves as compared to the way well-to-do persons and intellectuals would. We must be aware of what it means to have been, throughout one's history, defenseless in the face of structures that appear gigantic, mysterious, and completely anonymous. Read Kafka, not Brecht, in order to imagine what life is like for underprivileged workers. Can you imagine what it means never to be in the know, to be unaware of what is being planned, and to know that everywhere you will always be treated differently from everyone else? At the grocery store and in the cafe, they do not serve you the same way they serve others, and you sense it. To put up with all this and still use the existing structures requires tremendous courage when, all your life, you have learned that it is better to keep your head down and be quiet.

You asked me what the unions could do. They could have underprivileged workers meet with people who are capable of learning from them how to rebuild a workers' movement that would involve them, too.

7.

The Rough Roads
of Our Times

Gilles Anouil: We have discussed the Church and workers' movements. We shall soon have to start discussing the movement that you yourself created: the Fourth World Movement. But first, I would like to ask you one final question about what you term "a people." Where are they? Where should we look for them? Where are you going to lead us when you talk of your Movement?

Father Joseph Wresinski: I can only offer you an approximation or, if you like, a compass to discover the backroads of our time. We have said that the question of the underprivileged cannot be understood in geographical terms. It is a social, economic, and political situation. Underprivileged workers are found at the bottom of the social ladder. But where is the bottom of the ladder? It is everywhere, in all our cities and all over the countryside. Paths that lead that low are barely passable, so we don't see them.

We have never had the means to draw a map showing the distribution of the poor in France. It would, in any case, have to be a constantly changing map. I have told you about the way these families are expelled or displaced according to other people's convenience or according to the wishes and needs of neighboring housing projects, local authorities, or new companies. I have seen inhabitants of a shantytown rehoused or simply evicted for the sake of a park or a green space. This applies to most countries of the world: the poorest are always forced to leave the place they happen to be in. Whether they are chased by stones, bricks, or bulldozers, the story remains the same. The poorest have always been chased beyond the suburbs and banned from living in the housing areas of "decent people." This still happens today. The life of Christ also gives us some direction in this matter. Didn't he spend a great deal of his time fleeing on the roads of Galilee, Judea, and Samaria?

Fleeing, but where? Where can these families go?

I think the Fourth World has always been forced to settle, to congregate for a certain length of time in certain types of areas, urban or rural or even halfway between the two. The poor stayed in controlled areas like those around the Saint-Martin or Saint-Denis gates in Paris, or in areas of little economic interest or in a process of decay, or on vacant lots where no development had yet been planned. When very poor individuals and families settle in large numbers in a location, they soon inspire fear in other citizens. Then intimidation or "cleaning" operations start. The poor go away, either of their own accord or by force, and from then on they are "elsewhere," no one bothers to know where. The main goal was to empty the place, to make the community feel safe again, and to close the files. The expelled families continue to live underground until they congregate again somewhere. All this explains the lack of sure indicators. It took some time for the Movement to find out where the poorest live.

In France we see a population clustered at the outskirts of the cities; periodically they are pushed out into wider belts as urbanization spreads. You are familiar with the history of the former poverty zone around Paris. We retraced an almost identical history in Lyons, Caen, Rheims, and Marseilles. Everywhere, Fourth World families were forced to retreat in the same way, sometimes in such a hasty, panicky move that the authorities would think that, this time, they were really scattered for good. But some time later, they had an unpleasant surprise— the families were crammed together again in one location.

People condemned to living on scraps have no say in their housing accommodations, either. They go where their limited strength takes them, often without much consideration. Or they just go to a place from which they won't be evicted, such as a vacant lot, a shack built with their own hands, or a cellar. But the choice of location is limited because a very poor family cannot afford to become isolated from the world. In order to subsist, they need help and the presence of others. Then, sooner or later, there is another large concentration of families in areas with cheap lodgings.

Furnished rooms in Paris and other cities were at certain times the habitat of the poorest. When we look carefully, we find their ancestors in the "zones" around cities, which I have just described. Around Paris, this zone offered refuge to the very poor long before it was declared an area reserved for defense purposes. For a long time, the families who found shelter there earned their living by doing the most humble jobs in the city and also by working in quarries and gypsum deposits or by doing farm and seasonal work. All lived on the same vacant pieces of land.

In fact, did they have to stay in a given place because of their livelihood?

They were there because they couldn't get housing in the city and they were not welcomed in rural villages nearby. You are right, however, because if these families were left alone, they would not move once they had found a means of survival. In the past, the prospect of a job or of any way of earning some money could also lead the poor to take to the roads. During the boom in the naval trade, following great discoveries from Spain to the Dutch provinces, the very poor went to the harbors. Housing and job market regulations practically halted this mobility, at least for the poorest. In Western Europe, the migrant labor force is no longer made up of the very poorest, except perhaps in Spain and Italy. In order to migrate, one needs legal papers or else money for illegal migration. As for internal migration, it is becoming increasingly rare to find underprivileged workers harvesting and picking in the fields. Quite often they have been replaced by machines and by the work of young students.

In the past, almsgiving by abbeys and cathedrals could also influence the movement of the poorest. This is still the case in Muslim countries, with almsgiving at the mosques on Fridays. Beggars, peddlers, and fairground showmen would set off for Rheims, Tours, and Barcelona at the start of the winter. The possibility of refuge in asylums and general hospitals was passed on by word of mouth. At some point, Strasbourg Cathedral was forced to barricade its buttresses because of the number of poor people who were flocking to find shelter. The "people's kitchens" and the "soup kitchens" that have opened in our own time in Detroit, Amsterdam, and Paris are the vestiges of this ancient charity. They multiplied in the winter of 1982 to 1983, and the more numerous they were, the more the very poor and the homeless spread the word and found their way there.

Abbé Pierre is doubtless the most recent example of just such a pole of charity. The winter during which he raised his voice in protest was a big moment in the history of the Church. The love of Christ was made real through Abbé Pierre, with the last becoming the first and the rich becoming their servants. It must be noted that, at the same time, other priests and lay-people had started to gather the poor together. Poor people were speaking of Abbé Pineau in Tours. In the surrounding area, "going to Tours" meant going to see this man they trusted. There were people like him throughout the country, and Abbé Pierre was, one might say, their figurehead.

Seeing hundreds of families rushing to the gates of Paris was not, however, to the honor of the Church.

Could Christians have acted sooner and prevented the misery of the homeless? But what means did they have and who listened to the Church in that postwar period? I maintain that Abbé Pierre was able to gather in one single movement the many but scattered people of goodwill. He radiated an intensity of love, a just indignation that the right to housing was not being taken seriously, and a real determination to force the government to assume its responsibilities.

At that time, in one of my parishes in the Aisne area, one of the poorest families came to see me: they wanted to join Abbé Pierre. I must admit that my parishioners, who were overjoyed at the departure of these noisy neighbors and their numerous offspring, did not take long to collect money for the journey. Other priests did the same as I did. That explains why, once in the emergency housing camp myself, I found so many men and women who were familiar with the Church. Abbé Pierre had attracted a certain type of client, if I may say so: that of the Church's poor population. In the housing projects set up subsequently by the low-income housing office in Paris, I met significantly fewer people who had been to church.

Above all, public opinion and the government responded to Abbé Pierre's appeal. One way or another, the homeless were gathered into the emergency housing or transit housing that was built at the time and was to be built for many years afterwards. These were always constructed with the idea that the homeless would be there only temporarily.

Temporarily? Don't some of those emergency housing sites still exist? Hasn't it often been said that the only thing that lasts is what was made to be temporary?

The emergency housing sites have lasted and some still exist. There is no part of France where there isn't a so-called "Abbé Pierre" housing complex. These are lodgings which are always about to be destroyed and which are always repopulated. The families themselves have changed. In the beginning, the authorities thought they were housing families temporarily tried by misfortune, who didn't have housing because of a slowdown in the building industry in France. Persons who were homeless solely for this reason gradually found new houses in the years that followed. Those who remained were the destitute, who were unemployed and without resources. Some of the emergency housing became vacant, and local authorities sent in all the French or migrant worker families they didn't know what to do with.

Therefore, in the sixties, the local authorities were faced with groups of people they had not wanted. By that time I was already very committed to the struggle, not for housing but for the elimination of subhuman conditions. My memories of those years are painful. We went to interdepartmental meetings where there were endless discussions about the ideal number of families who could "be scattered in the semi-urban web." That was the jargon of the time. Sociologists or psychologists enlightened civil servants on the "tolerance threshold" of a housing project. Was it 5 percent, 10 percent, or 12 percent of "anti-social" families? How many "problem" households could be tolerated by a housing project planned for other citizens? That was the question for an expert to answer. In truth, the local authorities were, as always, looking for a way to scatter or to confine a problem population. I became aware, in these meetings, of what it meant for the poor not to be politically represented.

The rehousing couldn't, however, be accomplished without the agreement of the families?

No one asked them, and no one thinks of doing it now either. Fourth World families, then as now, are deprived of a free choice of housing. Even citizens who aren't poor do not always have an adequate choice. Underprivileged families have no freedom of movement or choice of housing whatsoever. We mustn't forget this when we want to know where to find them. These families aren't free to choose either location or type of housing. Public and private authorities impose degrading and humiliating lodgings on them. A mutual aid organization that had been requested to rehouse families from the Noisy-le-Grand camp talked to me about "infra" housing for "infra" families. That was in the sixties. In Tours, at the same time, the authorities built cramped apartments where inhabitants had to sleep on mattresses placed on a bed of cement. There were steel doors, and the wooden shutters were removed at the last minute to prevent the families from using them as firewood. For the last fifteen years, poor families have been sent even further away than before, some of them penned up in housing of the lowest standards, where they can be seen or heard as little as possible. Before urban renewal, they could be found in the poor sections of cities and towns, in furnished rooms and slum apartments, wedged between a railroad station and a slaughterhouse, or between a loading platform and a warehouse. After urban renewal, you can be sure to find them on a small piece of land between a canal and a highway, between a factory and a garbage dump, behind a cemetery, or alongside a railway line. The families stay there, often on a temporary basis, and their rent agreements contain unusual clauses. This is another detail to remember. Go to the town hall and inquire about housing with special occupancy status, and you will know where to find the most disadvantaged tenants.

This is the case for low-income housing projects that still exist. New constructions of the same type are no longer thought of. But as for those that remain, I cannot see how they would be destroyed in the near future. Their inhabitants are completely settled in. I would not dare yet to say why. Even the families who have just arrived and who have not experienced substandard living conditions for long, bring problems I had not known previously. These families seem to be more anxiety-ridden and less determined to fight their situation. It is as if material poverty, which was more severe in the past, had given underprivileged families the energy to survive that they no longer possess nowadays. This is only a feeling; one must be very cautious and not jump to hasty conclusions. All I mean to say is that I find this dullness and world-weariness in certain streets or projects in West Germany and in the Netherlands. There again, families seem to have gained in material resources but to have lost their vitality.

To the stock of old housing projects were added some privately owned, low-income lodgings, all too dilapidated to be offered to other tenants. But I think the policy is to scatter families in different places. Housing officials probably think they are doing disadvantaged families a favor by placing them in apartments where they will not be able to afford the rents in the long run. But it is also a way of making a problem disappear by getting rid of it temporarily. Building distant housing projects was a way of removing those families from sight; scattering them has the same effect.

Do you attempt to find them again?

Certainly; and in any case the families remaining on site tell us where to find them. They are often relatives or former neighbors. I believe, moreover, that you only need to live in low-income housing and to hear the conversations of neighbors, shopkeepers, and social workers to know where the Fourth World is. One thing has never changed since the shepherds of Bethlehem and throughout history. The poor are the "good poor." The most impoverished are by definition "bad poor" and are designated by other names: "lazy," "antisocial," not families experiencing problems, but "problem families." I have already told you about the usual experience a worker-priest would have: after accompanying a fellow worker back to his housing, he would find in the same apartment building a family in which no one is working. This might be a very disadvantaged family. All the priest needs to do is to listen to people talking to know where the most impoverished family lives.

Don't disadvantaged families congregate in greater numbers in the Paris area?

I don't think so, judging from recent history. Paris doesn't keep its most disadvantaged people. The capital spews them out. At best it tolerates migrant workers. I have witnessed real bargaining over the expatriation of a truly disadvantaged population that was discovered during the renovation of the center of Paris. The state intervened to pay for rehousing in neighboring boroughs. Now it is the boroughs' turn to do everything to get rid of these people. Some housing projects in the Paris area were almost entirely inhabited by very disadvantaged French families in the sixties. Now 85 percent of their tenants are migrant workers' families. Because they are more regular with their rent payments, some painting was done and other improvements were made. The reputation of the housing project hasn't improved, but the poorest have left.

When you want to know numbers, however, you pose a basic political problem. The Fourth World is like a political void. Who wants to know about it, and who cares about its size? The underprivileged population is a statistical misunderstanding rather than a simple error of calculation. It always appears under more general categories of people, where it is indistinguishable as such. Who wants to be faced with people who are out of work, in poor housing, with no resources and lacking an education? In giving global figures of categories and numbers, as did writers such as Lionel Stoléru, René Lenoir, and more recently Serge Milano and Robert Lion, the most desperate situations are covered over. Public opinion accepts this; no one demands to know who among us is not only homeless but also jobless, penniless, uneducated, sick, and without any political representation. Amid this general indifference, the state can take refuge behind the uncertainty of figures so as not to do anything.

Figures have, however, been put forward. The press has mentioned eight to ten million underprivileged in the EEC and two million in France.

The Movement made the estimates that appear in EEC documents. We drew them up carefully, using complex interpretations. Two million for France in 1971 was a deliberate underestimate. We wanted to avoid any exaggeration and any accusations of demagoguery. But today, the mass media repeat these same figures which have never been updated.

To tell the truth, what was the value in having any figures at all? Where are the poor; how many are they—were those really the most important questions? I learned to treat them more and more as trick questions, questions we hide behind so as not to ask ourselves about what these families tell us. Whatever their number, the main point is surely that they reveal our betrayals, denounce our trickery, and force us to be true to our beliefs. The real question is to recognize the changes toward which they are leading us. Limiting ourselves to mere numbers is a way of ignoring the struggle of the poor. This has hardly changed.

Have you tried to ascertain the presence of the Fourth World in the countryside?

The majority of deprived families are found in the outskirts of cities. But we also find them in nearly all the villages of France and most probably in all the market towns. The other day, near Poitiers, friends drove me to a dozen former lodgings of agricultural laborers. This is where farmers used to house their workers. The village is renting those lodgings to underprivileged families. Little islands of that type exist almost everywhere in France. In any case, most families have lived in several different villages. It can happen that each of the children in a household was born in a different village. Nowadays I see an increasing number of families trying to go back to a village where one of the spouses has maintained family ties. This is not necessarily the village where they were born; and often they didn't stay there. But it is a place where they have left relatives or acquaintances. I don't know the exact reasons for their return. Obviously they hope to find a welcome there, but they are often disappointed in that respect. It is often harder for a very poor family to be integrated in a village than to settle in a city.

It is still difficult to know the origins of these families. Are they urban or rural? They themselves cannot always reply immediately; often you have to patiently retrace the past together, because knowing only the place of birth is not enough. The families have often lived in many different places. They move around for years for fear that their children will be taken away from them, or because of evictions or threats from the neighborhood, or because of rent arrears or debts. Sometimes they settle in one of the housing projects we have spoken about. When the housing authority plans the demolition of that housing, the families are moved on to other housing projects that are also under the threat of being demolished. As they go through a series of temporary housing, one loses track of the families; they end up looking for a shelter themselves. They take refuge under the roof of a brother, a sister, or a friend; they settle in a shack hidden in a small wooded area; or they find an old garage that is sublet to them. It would seem that their number is increasing. However, since I have known them, the circuits they take as they wander from place to place are practically the same. They are the circuits of makeshift shelters that they have to invent or improvise because no housing has been planned by the national authorities for those below the poverty level.

So Abbé Pierre's campaign and its momentum throughout the country have not been successful?

Abbé Pierre was able to mobilize the country and make the authorities aware of their responsibilities. As a result of his action, no one would now deny that housing for everyone is an obligation of the state. For him, the emergency housing and the camp for the homeless in Noisy-le-Grand were really temporary housing. In any case, his stature and his charisma of "serving the most suffering first" pushed him into a universal struggle in which individuals (who were unjustly termed tramps or vagrants) would be the witnesses. He became their companion, and their voice was heard in all the corners of the earth. One should not forget that either.

The discovery of an entire people composed mainly of very poor families came later. Those families pushed the Fourth World Movement into finding its own specific path.

This leads us to Noisy-le-Grand and the camp created by Abbé Pierre.

This was a camp created by the Emmaus rag pickers; Abbé Pierre never intended for it to last for fifteen years. It was not even temporary housing. It was a sort of encampment of two hundred and fifty "igloos"; that is, Quonset huts with dirt floors and no electricity or water. The families were scheduled to stay there a few weeks while awaiting the construction of a temporary housing project.

The Noisy-le-Grand camp quickly became the symbol of a people too impoverished to be welcomed anywhere else. The families came from almost everywhere in France, mainly from the west, the center, and the north. They came from cities and rural areas; some were from the center of Paris. Just the fact that they accepted so precarious a lodging—the type that in France was normally used for animals—was in itself a sign. Other families who had come in after hearing of Abbé Pierre's campaign had not accepted it. Some less deprived families who had also landed there managed to find other housing in the years that followed. The others not only remained there, but they turned the camp into something Abbé Pierre could not possibly have predicted: a place of welcome where the most impoverished families of France continued to arrive.

Public opinion, however, had been awakened. Didn't the public grow indignant?

Public opinion did what we all do as regards the poorest. It acknowledged the situation and put the blame on the families. They came from all over France and had never been used to living as a community or in groups. They soon stood out because of their poverty and their ignorance. To top all this injustice, they were reproached for their lack of hygiene in an encampment where a few public taps provided the only water. The authorities reproached the families for not cultivating what were described as "gardens"—the few square yards of clay beside the huts. As if people who were in an appalling state of health could possibly use up their remaining energy on growing lettuce or geraniums in soil that was just lent to them for a few weeks. Their "garden" served as a dumping ground, an extension of the area on which women and children were packed together. The camp started looking like a vast garbage dump, and that was unforgivable in the eyes of the surrounding community.

In fact, everyone blamed the families for what was inflicted on them: lack of community spirit, lack of order, of harmony, and of cleanliness. If they lived in the mud, in a half-moon shaped shelter on hard-packed soil, it was their fault; they liked it and wanted it that way.

To blame them for their poverty and to treat them as "social cases" was made all the easier because these people could not justify their condition. They were not like other homeless people. They could not say they were the victims of a slow-down in a certain region or sphere of activity, nor were they elderly or victims of natural disasters. So on the list of common explanations for poverty in France, all that was left was mental sickness, emotional problems, or ill will. All these were attributed to the poor families. This caused the Noisy camp to be seen as something that happened by accident, a horde of social cases or "bad poor" unintentionally gathered together.

This was how I found the camp in 1956, the year in which my bishop proposed that I go to Noisy and tell him whether I wanted to stay there.

8.

The First Allies, or the Courage to Commit Oneself

Gilles Anouil: You arrived at the Noisy-le-Grand camp in 1956 and you stayed there. What gave you the idea of starting the Movement? At what moment did you decide to start an organization rather than continue an isolated project? And why?

Father Joseph Wresinski: In 1956, the two hundred and fifty-two families in the Noisy camp had no links with the parish. So the religious authorities asked several dioceses if they would allow a priest to go there. My bishop thought of me and told me, "Stay there as long as you like and leave when you like; you still belong to this diocese and you may come back to it at any time." I was leaving behind seven villages in the Aisne region; but I went back there on Sundays to celebrate Mass and to teach the religious education class. This continued for four months. But, as I have already told you, from my first contacts with these families, the thought came to me that I was dealing with a people. Undoubtedly, my experiences as a child, an apprentice, and a young worker, and then my years as a seminarian and a priest finally came together and made sense. As a child, I grew up in a working-class neighborhood bordering a poorer one. When I was in the seminary, I would go to a destitute section of Soissons whenever I could. I had known underprivileged workers in the basement of the Valentine paint business where I had worked. In my rural parishes I had come into contact with extremely poor families. I then became known as "the priest of the good-for-nothings." In Noisy-le-Grand, all this took on a meaning. I thought to myself: they are a people—the people of misery. What unites them is not a common project or a shared happiness, but their suffering. It brings them together, entraps and humiliates them.

Was it then that you thought of starting an organization?

Not yet. First I had to live among these families. Slowly, certain facts became evident to me. The first one was that of voluntary material poverty. From the start, the families compelled me to give away some of my belongings, something I would not have had the strength to do on my own. For instance, on a particular day in February 1957, a family sent by the city of Versailles turned up at the camp. The two parents and five children were all chilled to the bone and had no belongings. There was only one thing to do, and that was give them my blankets. I thought then that I would find some more for myself the following day or a little later. But things did not work out that easily, and I had to stay in a freezing shack in the middle of winter with just my cassock and my cape to cover myself.

I had already known material poverty when I was a country priest. During the first months after my arrival in the Dhuizel parish, I did not have much to eat. I had come there with little luggage, and for a long time I had to eat straight out of pots. Still, all this was only a slight inconvenience. There were always people around me ready to help me out. In Noisy the deprivation I experienced was genuine, because all the families who lived there suffered the same deprivation. I saw no escape. This explains why my feeling of solidarity with the people in the camp was so intense.

Then something else happened that impressed me deeply. I remember a woman who arrived at nightfall, alone with her five children—two sons and three daughters. I had nothing to offer them except half a Quonset hut, thirteen feet by fifteen. Accompanied by two men, I led them there. The woman didn't even glance at the hut with its dirt floor. Instead she stared at the sinister-looking faces of the two men, and a look of terror froze on her face as if she realized then that she was entering a world of despair from which she would never escape. I told her, "Listen, a thought came to me when I was looking at your children; I was trying to imagine what my mother would have done. I think she would have gone off with her children to city hall, and she would have stayed there with the kids and declared, 'I won't budge until you give me a place to stay.'" Thinking about my mother made me realize there was only one thing to do for all the families: Make society welcome the poorest into its midst. I paid for that family to stay at a hotel, but the idea of forcing society to take its responsibilities has never left my mind since that evening.

Wasn't there any organization that could have handled this matter?

There were twenty-seven organizations and institutions, but none except Emmaus fought to provide housing for the poorest. I felt that these organizations patronized the families. Abbé Pierre alone had the stature to accomplish this, but his physical strength had betrayed him. This, incidentally, made me realize how the fate of the poor depends more on individuals than on organizations. If just one person disappears, the little security they have can vanish.

In Noisy the families were being exploited by storekeepers who sold them food at a higher price than it cost in the town. They were also exploited by certain charitable organizations. One in particular would photograph the children after requesting the parents not to wash them and not to dress them neatly. The idea was to make them look pitiable and to use the photos for raising money. Like many others, the same charity handed out clothes, milk for the infants, and money; but, in fact, it was like handing out dishonor. There was also a soup kitchen which, in the midst of so much misery, did not make sense. Men and women carrying tin pots went a roundabout way to avoid passing by my shack, such was their shame and their realization of the shame I felt for them. "It's for my dog," they said when they happened to meet me. All these attempts to help were in fact ways of giving up on the families, of trapping them in this camp of suffering, and of refusing to do what should have been done. These gestures of help only added a little more every day to the poverty and humiliation of the families. This led me to the decision to start an association with the camp inhabitants. The absolute priority was to keep only the essential and worthwhile services while getting rid of the others.

Therefore, you founded the Movement with the poor themselves, didn't you?

What else could I have done? Don't imagine I was a precursor of the notion of participation. I was one of them and I belonged to their community. Like them, I was cold and hungry. They made fun of me because I did not take advantage of my position as a priest. For instance, one day I was sitting on the ground, and a woman accosted me and asked for money. I had nothing to give and I told her so. She then turned to the passers-by and started shouting, "Look at this priest who has nothing to give me!" To a man who had come to ask for some coal, I had to say that I was cold myself, that I had nothing to give him. He nearly knocked me out, but I was faster and knocked him to the ground, as a result of which I gained my reputation as a black belt.

To whom else could I have become allied? The situation I shared with the families was intolerable, not for any one factor, such as those I have just told you about, but because it went on and on. Had it lasted six months, it would have been bearable, but not after a year. At the end of two years, either I would have been revolted or I would have given up altogether and sunk to the bottom with the population. Our first association was born from that fear; it was a way of sharing the daily tragedy. In fact, everything that followed came to life in the same way—from reality, from an overflow of injustice, and from the fear of sinking together. Everything stemmed from a shared experience, never from a theory.

The idea of a volunteer corps followed almost immediately. Without this volunteer corps, born in the midst of misery in the Noisy-le-Grand camp, nothing could have been achieved. What could the families and I do, if men and women who wanted what we wanted—to destroy extreme poverty and its shame—had not come forward to join us? I felt a vital need for it, but I had no idea yet of how this corps of volunteers committed to the poorest was to come about.

Meanwhile the families were making specific demands on me, particularly regarding young children. We couldn't possibly let them wade in the mud, suffer from dehydration in the summer, and fall ill in the winter. Everything essential for survival was lacking: food, clothes, and coal. There was no question of doing away with the soup kitchen and the distribution of clothes if we could not replace them with an overall program for fighting extreme poverty. However, to start a kindergarten, a secondhand clothing store, and a campaign to acquire coal, entailed the support of other people and an organization, which meant gaining the approval of the families and getting outside help.

Already in 1957, a few people from the camp had formed a "Family Office" because they did not want that type of life to continue. The first association was created with them. Some unknown intuition made us adopt the name "Group for European Action and Culture." We were founding exactly that—

an international association for the defense of human rights. But we were not aware of it then. What exactly did we envision in this camp which attracted utterly deprived families during that very cold winter of 1957–1958? At the least, we all had the strong feeling that we had to break the isolation. As Europe was a frequently mentioned topic in those years, calling ourselves a European action group was probably a way of being part of a larger current of thought, of escaping the dependency on aid by joining those who defended human rights. As for me, this was no doubt a concrete way of saying, "One day these families will climb the steps of the Vatican, UNESCO, the Elysée Palace, the UN, and the ILO."

But what strength, what power could the inhabitants of the Noisy camp have? Was not your venture doomed to failure from the start?

Very soon I knew we could not achieve anything alone. The association had hardly been established when I was summoned to police headquarters for questioning. Among the members of our organization were former prisoners who had in some cases lost their right to vote. What kind of plot was I preparing? An association of criminals, of insurgents? Our application to incorporate was denied. I had to find at least a few people who had never been in trouble with the police. I turned to a Protestant friend of mine, and we founded a new association. My friend requested that it be called "Aide à Toute Détresse."[12] The families agreed to this name, since our objectives would not change.

What were those objectives?

To dismantle the camp, to seek proper housing and, for those who wanted to do so, to return to other regions. Another objective was to understand life, to learn more about what was happening and who we were. We had not yet acquired the language we now possess. We could not foresee the whole range of tasks we would have to undertake later on. We did not know what was in store for us if we were to let ourselves be guided by life and remain faithful to our determination to put an end to injustice. However, I believe that the Movement was already present in those objectives; we wanted to work together for better living conditions. We also wanted to create opportunities for cultural activities and to build solidarity with the outside world in order to give existence to this people, and allow it to take its rightful place in the history and the future of humankind.

We began by installing water spigots (there were only about ten for more than two hundred and fifty families). We covered the dirt floors with concrete in a number of huts and installed electricity; we lined the walls of other huts and laid water pipes. At the same time, we opened the first centers of learning; that is, a kindergarten, a library, and finally a family center. Indeed, concern for the family is the basis of our Movement and the starting point of all its action. Destitution brings to light the absolute need to have the security of family life. In the camp at Noisy, this need was crucial because the family was threatened from all sides and broken up by interventions from outside; the parents had to defend themselves fiercely. Besides that, fire was a constant threat. The first family center, which we had installed in one of the huts, burned down on the day of its inauguration. We started building a new one in the months that followed.

Already the families showed perseverance, whereas the Ministry of the Interior still withheld its approval. We existed, not illegally (since we did no harm) but outside the law. I knew we were at the start of a long struggle. To assert the dignity and security of the families, we had to lay the foundations for the three following objectives: to live in a humane environment; to develop intellectually and spiritually; and to be recognized by the community at large.

But what could you do without an official status and without financial means? By acting without approval, didn't you bring more difficulties upon yourself?

We had to run the risk, since it was impossible to do nothing. We opened a bank account and hired an accountant. Mrs. Fouchet, a mother from the camp, kept the book of receipts and expenses after her day's work. I myself started to send appeals for funds in which I wrote about the suffering and the dignity of the families. These appeals had a real impact and helped to make the public aware of the persistence of destitution. Thus a support movement was formed. The only person I knew in Paris was a Ms. Lucille Sumpt, an elderly lady whom I had met by chance at the Cîteaux Abbey. She was the daughter of a general and had been a social worker in the 15th district of Paris between the two wars, when tuberculosis was still endemic among the poor. She opened the doors of many well-to-do families for me.

Did this mean I had reverted to the tradition of the rich giving charity to the poor? Certainly this was not what we wanted. In fact, the rich began to take risks for the sake of the poor. The camp was already too well known: the families had a bad reputation, and many charitable organizations had turned against us. Indeed, it was not by chance that the Ministry of the Interior had refused to approve our action. People needed to have a certain spirit of independence and the ability to see things from a higher level in order to commit themselves to helping us. Do not forget that Abbé Pierre's revolutionary message had not been favorably received in the Paris region. He said that people had to change the way they viewed the very poor, and this would necessarily entail a change in the structure of society. But this was not what Paris remembered and, once Abbé Pierre had left, Emmaus continued to run its soup kitchen. The families knew that more had to be done, but others did not appreciate them for saying so.

Many people thought you were part of Emmaus and that you subsequently went your separate ways.

In reality, my bishop had placed me at the disposal of the families in the camp; I was never part of Emmaus. But of course by going to Noisy, I was turning to Abbé Pierre, as in previous years I had turned to Abbé Godin and Abbé Depierre in my search for the victims of exploitation and oppression. To me, these men represented a great hope for the poor, and I was proud of a Church able to produce men of such stature. I felt I was the heir to this Church overflowing with love for the poorest. As a young country priest, I was nurtured by these priests who had chosen to be witnesses, to be a living protest to the situation of the oppressed.

Let us look back once more at the recent past. Imagine what the fifties meant in France for the poor. Since the war the housing situation was terrible. Whatever habitable housing was left had been taken by people who were better off, leaving the poorest to survive in dreadful conditions. The mechanization of agriculture had caused many to flee from the country to the cities, where the labor market was not active enough to provide work for these migrants. Politicians were preoccupied with other matters, and public services pretended not to know that destitution existed. Not to mention the wars in Indochina and Algeria, from which many men returned in ill health, with no job and no future. (The army and the Foreign Legion had long been a refuge for the poor in France.) Around 1955 and 1956, hundreds of children were malnourished.

This state of affairs could not last without some people rising up against it all. Abbé Pierre was one of the key figures of these protests. But he did not have enough time to size up the situation. He discovered large families with children sleeping in the open and, thanks to men like Périer-Daville,[13] he launched an extensive and persistent campaign to denounce society for not coming to the aid of people in danger. As I said before, Abbé Pierre was struck down by illness before he could see his discovery through. The families, however, will never forget his message.

Was your ambition to fill a gap and change the course of events?

That was not the point; we had to carry on what Abbé Pierre and others had done. Families were being crushed by poverty, and the authorities pretended not to notice it. Children were scrounging for food in garbage cans; others were walking half-naked in the streets, in the cold of autumn. More than one third of school-age children did not attend school. The majority of the fathers were unemployed, and the mothers made extreme sacrifices. Some women became prostitutes on Saturday nights to earn a few francs to buy food for their children. Yet the authorities accused us of exaggerating.

I am deeply convinced that our Movement could not help but exist once the situation of the families had been exposed. The families' state of abandonment in Noisy—which soon after also became apparent in emergency housing projects—had to give rise to new initiatives and to a new analysis of the situation. Someone had to proclaim that destitution was a global issue and involved an entire population of families. It was a social stratum which, in fact, included adults, children, old folks, and isolated individuals. The Movement had to happen: the history of the poorest was the motivating force. The time had come when they would be able to question society at large, to contest it, and to challenge it at its core. A sort of union occurred then between a desperate population and a group of men and women who refused to accept the despair of their brethren.

We were inspired by what happened. A very odd alliance was created between a discredited population and a group of rich people in Paris who did not think they were accountable to anyone. I often think about this, and I believe a lesson must be drawn from it. These Parisian personalities—for example, a high-ranking official in the Organization for European Cooperation and Development and other well-known people—probably initially thought they were getting involved in some ordinary aid program. Actually, they soon found that they were risking their credibility. Not only were they defending an indefensible population, but also, through their initiatives, they were offending existing charitable organizations. Some of them were worried and were wondering whether they had been fooled. They were antagonizing well-established institutions, some of which were run by their own families or friends. They were concerned about the outcome of risking their credibility in this way in the eyes of their own people. They even received threats.

Respectable people in such an awkward position vis-à-vis their peers—could it last for long?

Some abandoned us. Others have become staunch friends. All, I believe, have learned humility. They had thought they were influential and free from slander. After siding with the poor, they realized it was not at all obvious, especially as administrative decisions concerning the poor are usually made at a low level. The civil servant from the Ministry of Health who had power over the fate of the families in the camp at Noisy was not a high-ranking official. Such power vested in subordinate officials was all the more dangerous as there was no political control, even in the long term. Our democratic institutions were not interested in a population so severely lacking in "efficiency" (a term often used then). Consequently, persons used to dealing with government ministers and chief executive officers suddenly felt very awkward when confronted with junior officials who were often full of good will but lacked competence and vision. Once, a member of our board of directors, who was second to the head of a major airplane manufacturer, was ordered by an official at the Ministry of Health to leave his office immediately, otherwise he would be thrown out by a guard. He then went out of his way to meet a low-ranking civil servant and invited her to dine in a restaurant she might never have known if the camp for homeless people had not existed. I have witnessed many seemingly comical situations, and today we laugh as we remember them. However, we did not feel at all like laughing at the time. These affluent people, who were used to security and prestige, were unprepared for the slanders they were now subjected to along with the poor families.

Today, the "allies"—as we refer to the active members of the Movement—are defined by shared disgrace. But now they know it and are prepared for it. The first allies had to learn everything the hard way, being looked upon with disapproval by their peers without always knowing why.

I find it difficult to imagine these people coming to the camp. Did they meet the families?

Yes, they came to the camp and met the families. Things were simple in those days. Nobody could come and see me without meeting the people at the same time, as they were all around me. Some of our friends from Paris came to Mass. At first we prayed in one of the huts. Then we built a chapel.

But the fact of coming to the camp and witnessing such glaring poverty entailed another danger for these friends. How could they avoid becoming like all the others dispensers of money, clothes, and food? The temptation was strong, for how was it possible not to give in the face of so much destitution? However, we do not want to humiliate people by distributing alms; we can only give our own selves and our own lives. The greatness of the Movement allies has been and still is the fact that they do not seek a way out by handing out material goods. Rather, they accept that the volunteers who devote their lives are in the forefront.

What stays in my memory concerning those friends is their act of faith. I cannot find a better word to describe their trust. They could see the families in the grip of the greatest misery. They could hear their cries. They could smell the odor of destitution. They could see me, a priest, in my threadbare cassock. They could see how, in the middle of vespers, I was dragged out to put a stop to a fight and received blows myself in the process. They came to pray in the chapel and were disturbed by the children who were pushing and shoving each other. During my sermon, a man would interrupt to show his approval. All this could have been disconcerting for people used to the streets of the exclusive 16th district in Paris and the fervent atmosphere of the Spanish church in the rue de la Pompe. But they never said a word. There existed between us an agreement and a deep mutual trust, which made any explanation superfluous.

Was it with these people that you were eventually able to create a recognized movement?

The time for this came later, with the strengthening of the volunteer corps. With our friends, we founded an association that was in accordance with the not-for-profit organization law. We needed a courageous person to be its president. That person was André Etesse, an assistant to the executive director of a major industry. That was in 1960.

André Etesse had heard about the camp through an article in a weekly magazine. He first came on July 14, 1960, to leave a package of clothing. I saw him get out of his car and, without waiting to hear what he wanted, I asked him to help me in a matter of great urgency. A few hours earlier a man had died; he was lying on a bedstead in the stifling heat, and his back was already eaten by worms. I asked André Etesse, "As you have a car, could you go and get the medical examiner? We cannot find him anywhere." He did what I asked, then he went to see the mayor to arrange for the man's burial. In the meantime, he helped me carry the body to the chapel, since we could not leave it in the hut, with his children around. We had to wait several days for the funeral to take place because the local authorities refused to pay for it. I celebrated Mass in the chapel. André Etesse was there; he saw the rats scampering about the body.

Here was a man who had come to leave some clothing and who was confronted with a misery that hunted a man even to his coffin. The next day, I asked him to become president of our association. He first sought his wife's agreement because he realized he was committing himself to something out of the ordinary. And so, thanks to the dead man whom the local authorities refused to bury, we found our first president. This was the beginning of public life for the families and for the volunteer corps.

Were there other allies like him?

The number of members increased fairly rapidly, each person bringing new ones. One of the first to join was Mrs. de Brancion, a friend of Ms. Sumpt and of Geneviève de Gaulle. When Geneviève saw the lines of huts and the camp frozen by cold in the winter of 1958, she thought she was back in the Ravensbrück concentration camp, where she had been interned during the war. Geneviève, too, has stayed with us ever since. Today she is the president of the Movement in France.

When I consider these first allies, one by one, I detect in them two common characteristics. They were not what one might call do-gooders; that is, people already active in charitable organizations. Nor did they play an official role in the Church. This explained their total lack of prejudice, of preconceived ideas such as more informed people might have had. Our allies had, as it were, no past regarding the challenge that the camp at Noisy represented for them. This gave them much simplicity, responsibility, and sincerity. The same could be said of the first volunteers, the ones who built the volunteer corps. As for me,

I was totally ignorant of all that concerned structures, legal questions, and the complexities of a well-organized public life.

You do not seem to take kindly to people committed to charitable organizations?

That is not the point. The Fourth World required untried things from us. We had to be like a blank page on which the families could write what they had to say. We had to be penetrable, to have a ready ear at all times, and to accept the fact that the families were our masters. Our allies had no preconceived ideas. Some, like Roger Siot, were engineers. They judged according to actual evidence, not according to some doctrine. They were broadminded and not prisoners of a theory.

But I did not intend to say that we did not have very good friends in existing institutions. Quite the contrary. However, the existence of so destitute a population confronted them with difficult questions. Or was it perhaps that our frail association challenged them by the very way it behaved? In spite of our frailty, we gave them a feeling of insecurity. For we questioned anything that had been established without taking the poorest into account, and we did not provide any answers. Today we may have some ideas concerning the direction in which institutions can seek answers. But back in the sixties, we had enough trouble merely existing. All we had to offer was our constant questioning. Friends from other organizations did not always find this sufficient motive to stay with us.

Didn't you attract institutions such as Catholic Action or the Young Christian Workers' Association?

Some of their members stayed with us in a personal capacity, but the time for alliances with other institutions came much later. The merit of the first ones who stayed with us is all the greater. They were torn between an old allegiance and a new commitment. Some left their former organizations to join us. I witnessed real heartbreaks during those years, and I still see some today.

Thinking back, it seems that what united those who remained so strongly was their attachment to the families. In Noisy and the other subsequent housing projects we went to, the last refuge for a person was quite evidently the family. It was the last line of defense against adversity, humiliation, and self-destruction. It was the final irreducible cell. Soup kitchen distributions and our clumsy acts of mutual aid could not destroy it entirely.

It took the Church some time to rediscover the family.

The Church doesn't rediscover the family; it has always had Jesus' family as an example (especially the family put to flight). The Church is this family, which is hunted down because it is vulnerable.

In any case, what united us—believers and non-believers—was the fact that we did not accept the destruction of the family. You know what was said in those days and it is still said today: "Nothing more can be done for the parents, but it is still possible to save the children." This idea of saving the children by destroying the parents and the home is unbearable.

During those first years, the idea of the family made us hold on together. The notion that the poorest formed a people was already important to the volunteers and a number of our first allies, but not to most of our friends. "If they are a people, it makes all the difference," someone told me one day. He meant that it changed everything in his own life; he had to rethink all his former attitudes and actions. Not all the Movement's friends made this discovery. They had not reached that level of awareness in the early sixties, when we began to have an increase in the number of members. We were linked together because of the intolerable misery that broke up the family and made love impossible.

I can see it when I read the appeals I wrote in those times and re-read old letters. I have kept a lot of them because the Movement was built up through letters and personal correspondence. Of course, a priest is taught to respect every individual as a special person, and that was probably reflected in the way I wrote my letters (often at night until early morning, helped by Mrs. Fouchet and Mrs. Paget). Very soon, I received many letters to which I replied personally. I did not consider this a duty. To me, every new correspondent was a potential friend. I could not act otherwise for the sake of the families. For them, every potential supporter was indispensable. This is still true. Consequently, the Movement functions on a very personal level, or "personalized" as the term is today. People of a whole generation—even several generations—express themselves through those letters. Looking back, I am struck by the way people reacted to what I wrote to them about the families.

Today the Church is renewing its defense of the family. In my opinion, this concern never left it, even when it dared not speak of the family as it does today. Moreover, I do not think anyone could be unconcerned about it. In any case, since 1957, the friends who are faithful to the Movement are those who believe in the family, whatever their religious or political convictions. It may be that the idea of the family could in itself have constituted a sufficient basis for our struggle. I cannot say, because another conviction was already shared by a number of us; that is, the families were to be seen as a people for whom it was worth taking a stand, a people in serious need of a corps of volunteers committed for life.

9.

"Put Out Into the Deep and Lower Your Nets for a Catch"

Gilles Anouil: Let's talk about the volunteer corps. You created it, and Fourth World volunteers are close to your heart, as much as the families, I believe. Yet you speak of them as if they were separate from you: "They did everything... It is thanks to them that we were able to do..."

Father Joseph Wresinski: It is true I called them, but they forged themselves into a volunteer corps. When I was ordained, I chose as a motto "Put out into the deep and let down your nets for a catch." For me, that meant I was not going just anywhere. "Put out into the deep" means to head out for the open sea, and then "let down your nets." To immerse myself at Noisy and completely throw my lot in with the poor was, in a way, doing the opposite. It was probably against my nature. In my case, even if I sincerely wanted to do it, God knew better and decided otherwise. He led me to bear witness and to call for volunteers in all countries.

On the one hand being immersed among the people, and on the other hand heading for the open sea, is less contradictory than one might think. I had really immersed myself in the poverty of Noisy-le-Grand and asked the first volunteers to do the same. But the genuine will to go as far as possible with so poor a people led me to understand that it is not possible to die with the poorest unless this death is transformed into their resurrection. They themselves have to become messengers for humanity. In fact, being immersed in such a destitute place, empty-handed and defenseless, forced me more than ever to "head out for the open sea."

You called for volunteers; they came and followed in your steps. Why do you say they forged themselves into a corps of volunteers?

They answered my call; but I was separate from them, and they had to build themselves up. I didn't come from the same place they came from. I could tell them about the life and the way of thinking of the poor, but they had to rebuild their lives and their thoughts accordingly. I could give them leads, but they had to take the initiative. I could not even give them enough space to let them find their way; I was always unsettling them. They had scarcely arrived when I had to tell them to head out to the open sea in their turn and make a start in other destitute areas. They could not keep to themselves, form their little clique, or isolate themselves. Heading out to the open sea means living under a tent and being exposed to the elements. It also means living in the midst of men and women with very different social backgrounds, ages, and beliefs. Can you imagine what it means to build a volunteer corps in such conditions?

I want to stress that they did build up this volunteer corps and that they had no one to help them and no models to refer to.

Your approach in calling for a volunteer corps with people from different faiths is a contradiction for two reasons. First, when you say the Church is the church of the poor, one cannot understand why you founded a volunteer corps outside the Church. Second, how do you reconcile your appeal to people of all beliefs with the problem of destitution, which necessarily calls not only for action, but also for an ideology?

Things are simpler if you look at them from the point of view of the poorest and of people in general. To see a volunteer corps of all denominations and ideologies being formed is a fundamental human need. Not only is it a need, but it is also a right—the right of the most disadvantaged to be at the center of all creeds and ideologies and the right of all people to be united in spite of their differences. By creating a movement where all could meet, I am convinced I acted in the name of the Church, according to Jesus' prayer to the Father, "That they may all be one." It was not an easy thing to understand— not for me, not for the volunteers, and not for others who were watching us. To tell the truth, I believe that only the families could understand it. The fact of acting within the Church while building something at its side, and of wanting the corps thus founded to belong fully to all, implied a boundless trust in human beings, a trust that had to be contagious. The Church had trusted me, and by letting myself be led by it, one day I found myself building outside its walls. I was in a no-man's land; I was leading others there, and we had not much around us to draw upon.

Even while acting outside the Church, all the same, you were helping to build it up?

I hope so. But in the Movement, others were building with me according to their own ideas and beliefs. From the start we were and, I hope, shall always be, strictly on an equal footing. Christians seek to be fully committed to their faith by identifying with Christ's suffering. Others are as fully committed to what they think and hope for. What unites us and transcends our differences is our choice of the same witness to our sincerity. The poorest are witnesses not to our reason and intelligence but to our sincerity, and therefore to our quality as human beings.

In the Movement, we are not experts in ecumenism. We try to live out our unity from day to day, not through the contents of faith but by being sincere, by going as far as we have to in our personal commitment to the poorest. Unity has to be the outcome, since it is found where the most deprived families are. By focusing our efforts on them, we are all sure to become united and equal.

This idea of a platform where all people of good will could meet came to me as soon as I arrived in Noisy. Christians don't always realize how fortunate they are to have been taught from the cradle not so much to serve others but to be in communion with others. As children, they learn to see others as themselves. They also learn that service, solidarity, and commitment are not enough, but that they must give of themselves in order to let others grow.

Is this specific to Catholics?

It is a special sensitivity of theirs, a chance offered to them but to which all are entitled. In the Movement and in the volunteer corps, each one is welcomed as he or she is, and each one shares what he or she is with the others. What counts is the sincerity of the people. No one is supposed to give lessons to others, but everyone must be ready to be taught by the same master. To make the poor one's masters is not just a requirement for the Church. The Fourth World volunteer corps endeavors to make this the measure of its authenticity.

You can say that today, after twenty-five years of experience. But what did you say to the first volunteers?

All we could say and do has been dictated by the lives of the families. We had to live and we had to react to the realities of their lives. After that, we were in a better position to explain things to ourselves. At the beginning we simply shared the will to be united around the families and with the families. Our unity stemmed from the realization that being united with the families without being united among ourselves did not make sense. The need of the Fourth World for a corps of volunteers was so palpable and so obvious that such a corps had to become a historic reality.

The first volunteers were young women. In those early days, it was necessary to have a lot of love, to be willing to take many risks, and to be forward-looking—able to guess not only the suffering endured by the families but also their future, that of the parents and children. For the sake of the future, which could only be imagined and hoped for, we had to renounce many things and run the risk of failure. The families and friends of the first volunteers did not hesitate to voice their thoughts: "You're wasting your life. There's no future in what you're doing." The volunteers had no answer to that, no proof to the contrary. Their commitment was a wager on people and on life. This called for an imagination and creativity out of the ordinary. Perhaps for this reason, it wasn't until 1965 or 1966 that male volunteers came to join us, when the time of the greatest dangers had passed.

As for these women, they were very different from one another in their social and cultural backgrounds, their beliefs, and their nationalities. Each of them lived a full life in society; they were all used to having responsibilities and working with other people. They never let themselves be trapped in rivalries, conflicts between people, or abstract discussions. Day after day, they laid the foundation of the volunteer corps, and they created the Movement.

I told you that these young women were of various nationalities. Bernadette was French; Erika, German; Francine, Belgian; and Alwine de Vos,

Dutch. It was Bernadette Cornuau, the French woman, who forced us to become really and truly united. Not only did she not believe in the Church, she could not even stand the Church—and I was a priest. She volunteered to come on Saturdays and Sundays, and she also devoted her holidays to the children of the camp. Like all the other volunteers, she took some time before deciding to leave her job and come and live as part of the team. For her, as for everyone else, joining the volunteer corps was a trial. No one knew what to expect in those early days, but they all had some intuition. Because of her sense of loyalty, Bernadette took her time to make a commitment to the Movement. She told me, "I cannot stay because, first of all, I am in love and I have to live my own life. Also, you are a priest and I have no religious faith; I am not for the Church. When the children speak of religion to me, I have to tell them honestly what I think. Therefore I am contradicting you." I told her then that it was important for the children to meet sincere people with different but complementary and uncompromising opinions. Yet, like every one of us, Bernadette first sought to escape. She agreed to be sent to England by her company. Then, one day, without any warning, she came back, leaving behind family, love, and career to join us.

Bernadette is still the one who personifies respect for other people's opinions; even more, she personifies trust in those who think differently, to the point of leaving your future in their hands. In effect, joining the nascent volunteer corps meant, from the start, putting your life not only at the mercy of the poorest but also of other volunteers who did not share your way of thinking. It meant losing your hold on any kind of security. You do not always realize the trust that is needed and the risks that have to be taken when you accept to share your life with people who think differently. In a way, it is like surrendering yourself, giving yourself up completely, and putting yourself in a situation comparable to that of the poorest. Perhaps this is why the volunteer corps has attracted so much admiration and, at the same time, so much discredit.

You spoke about Bernadette Cornuau. Who were the others?

Erika Wandelt is a German Lutheran who earned a doctorate in linguistics. She was eighteen and had come to France to improve her French; she arrived one afternoon at the camp. After that, for two years she spent all her vacation time with us. Then she became frightened and did not return. Yet, after completing her studies, she joined the volunteer corps. Two years later, she married and moved with her husband to a place that was absolute hell—an abandoned military barracks in Rastatt, which housed families labeled "asocial" (as they were also labeled in France at the time). The German authorities allocated to these families a type of lodging that was supposedly provisional. While living there, Erika had two children and converted to Catholicism. She died from cancer some years ago. But up to the end, true to her way of doing everything in peace and joy, she had family files brought to her bedside. By keeping records up to date, she knew she was contributing to the history of the families and to their liberation.

There was also Francine Didisheim from Belgium, whose father was a Jew and who carried within her the Jewish identity and culture. Francine was a convert to Catholicism, as was Alwine de Vos from the Netherlands, who was one of the first women to be a diplomat in her country. Each of these volunteers had her own distinctive character and spirit of independence. They all had to break with a good deal of their past without being able to give much explanation to their relatives and friends. The volunteer corps and the Movement were still to be founded. These women were leaving their surroundings and their careers, but for what and to go where? They needed strong convictions not to be swayed by the opinion of others and to face hostility and lack of understanding. I cannot think of these first volunteers without feeling an immense affection and deep gratitude to them.

How could these women give up their careers and lifestyles without explaining clearly that they were choosing another way of life? How did they justify the step they were taking?

They didn't. There was no acceptable justification except that of the families. I told you these families were gathered in Noisy, not with a view to the future, but because of their destitution and suffering. The families' suffering was the only motivation for the first volunteers and for those who came later, until 1968. Up to that time, they were all welcomed in the camp at Noisy; we had no suitable place elsewhere. I am not saying that all those who came wished to become volunteers and stayed. Hundreds of adults and teenagers came and went. Those who remained as volunteers were, I think, people deeply affected by suffering. It is not possible to tolerate the prolonged misery of people close to you without reacting. Either you reject them because they have become unbearable, or you make their suffering your own, sharing it with them in order to destroy it.

I am thinking of a Belgian teacher, Gabrielle Erpicum. She first came to spend an afternoon there on the first of November. She was mistreated by a group of children for whom she had tried to organize activities. They insulted her and threw stones at her. She went back to Belgium. Upon reflection, however, she decided she could not continue to benefit from all the things she had received—family, affection, faith, and education—without sharing them with young children who could never be offered even the smallest amount of these precious gifts by their own parents, hounded as they were by extreme poverty. What motivated her, and all the first volunteers, to stay was a refusal to accept such injustice: Why me? Why not them? They wanted to go all the way. As the gospel says: "What was given to you as a gift, give it also as a gift, without profit." In fact, without a revolution, the volunteers had initiated the prototype of a society in which our first duty is to give back to others what we have received, the prototype of the profitless society. This is what Mary Rabagliati meant when, having come to Noisy at the age of nineteen, she refused to return to London because she did not want to spend her life earning money.

With the Fourth World, there is only one choice. Either we reject and exclude from our lives those whose situation, ignorance, and behavior are becoming intolerable; we do not recognize them as human beings and might even exploit them, which is just another way of refusing to see them as brothers and sisters. Or we refuse to squander what has been given to us by our family, our society and our social environment, our friends and God. To allow those who have received nothing to blossom is a way of gaining as we lose, because we reap an increased amount of love, which in turn is also a gain for them. We wish them to receive what we have received, and more if possible. We no longer want to take advantage of the situation that was offered to us. We want to give without any thought of being paid back. This will to restore justice is no utopia. The volunteer corps is based on just such a will, and struggles for that kind of justice.

Those who become volunteers have rights, which are fully recognized and which they can claim. But they can also use these rights for the benefit of others—for those families in low-income housing, those unemployed men who have nothing to do all day long, those fathers whose children are hungry and whose wives endure unending misery. All these people are denied their rights, and this deprivation proves that rights are not founded exclusively on a human being's existence. Nor does the mere fact of existing suffice for such people to recognize that they have rights as human beings. Each person must justify these rights for themselves. Not only do the volunteers expose that situation, but also they turn it upside down. They use their liberty and their rights to assert the priority of the poorest in its life, in the life of the volunteer corps. This is the same approach I described earlier. We do not share the suffering of the underprivileged without sharing their hopes, without wishing to see their suffering cease and their situation change—and change immediately. There is no question of dying with them without being instrumental in their resurrection. I think that the volunteer corps, through its very existence and through its action, provides the foundation and the realization of rights for the poorest. At the same time it is at the origin and the heart of a vision for a new society. It is also starting to realize this vision.

What you are saying sounds rather abstract. Can you tell us what actually takes place in the lives of the families? What do the volunteers do concretely?

Very often the families expect us to be educators or social workers. There is no question of disappointing them; so we undertake some programs that correspond to their expectations. We set up pre-schools, medical centers, cultural centers, vocational training programs, and literacy courses. "Tapori," the children's branch of the Movement, was the outcome of such initiatives, as was the youth movement with its discovery clubs. Meetings, demonstrations, and various events where the families could express themselves, get used to public speaking and debating, were the by-products of trade union activities.

These programs ensure that our own heritage becomes that of others. The desire to see families practice their rights is necessarily sealed by concrete action in the midst of people in the Fourth World, but also in and with society at large. Indeed, we are led to do three things simultaneously: to denounce the denial of rights; to re-establish them ourselves; and to oblige others to admit to the poorest that they have such rights. Our approach is always twofold. You and we are among the "haves;" they are the "have nots." You and we are recognized; they have no representation anywhere. The questions are: What are we going to do, and what are you going to do with us so that they can obtain justice? We have more than we need. What are you going to do with us for those families who will be sitting at an empty table tonight, so that they may have the basic necessities of life? Our children attend the university. What are we doing, you and I, so that their children, who cannot even read or write, can learn a trade? If all we do is denounce a situation to others, it has no impact. We also have to take initiative to show that the eradication of extreme poverty is possible. Our Movement initiates programs so that others, in turn, may do the same. This is why the Movement carries on pilot projects to prove that the restoration of rights is possible. The families who aspire to have their rights recognized commit themselves in turn to obtain this recognition themselves. All the Movement's programs within the population amount to asserting the rights of people, for the families, for the volunteer corps, and for society at large. They denounce injustice by restoring justice and by proving that justice is possible.

I said one day that the Fourth World was a fragment of the Eucharist because it continuously re-enacts Christ's passion and resurrection. Indeed, it never ceases to bear witness to human beings' determination to survive the worst setbacks and to proclaim their dignity. The Fourth World has a thousand ways of repeating again and again that no one, however destitute, is content to be unable to share with others and to be excluded from political, religious, and cultural life. I have never known anyone who would accept being considered inferior. Human beings are not asking for a symbolic respect without concrete content; they do not want to be "christified," if I may say so. They want an education for their children, a place where they can live autonomously, and a real job that gives them an identity as workers so that they can say, "I am a bricklayer, a sheet metal worker. I am socially useful, and consequently I have a political role to play." Sharing the suffering of the poorest has led us to struggle for the effective recognition of their rights.

You could not possibly have had such a program back in the years when you started in Noisy?

I remember, very early on, we used to say to the first volunteers: We must live according to a certain type of society and in that way be witnesses to the type of society that we learn from the families. They were teaching us two things. We had to continually let go of certain things in order to be enriched in other ways; and we had to search for a lifestyle, a way of being together that would indicate a different kind of society.

From then on, we concentrated our action on the family and on everything that could strengthen it. As I was telling you, right from the start we wanted to be a family movement, a movement carrying the families' hopes and their deep aspirations for mutual love. We met with a lot of antagonism from society at large, because it was becoming increasingly suspicious of the family in general and of those families in particular. For us, the point was not to lay a wager on the family per se. The volunteers believed in its value; they were convinced, from seeing it with their own eyes, that it was impossible to liberate the Fourth World without reasserting the value of the family. That statement is so true that the expression "the families" is now part of the volunteers' vocabulary, referring to the entire underprivileged population. We might say it was the first term in a language we slowly developed. "The families" implied the poorest, the underprivileged, and the Movement.

It is true that a special kind of language is used within the Movement. In fact you are criticized for it and accused of all speaking the same way. "Whether you hear one or the other, they all say the same thing...."

This is true as far as a certain number of basic options are concerned, but it should not surprise anybody, given the rather uncommon situation in which we found ourselves. Some people listening to us may find this unsettling when they realize that our beliefs sometimes go against the current of public opinion.

Apart from our preferential concern for the family, our statement of basic beliefs stipulates priority of the poorest. This means more than just giving priority to the Fourth World in our own lives. Within the Fourth World, the most downtrodden, the most broken and the most despised family will be the cornerstone of the presence and efforts of a team of volunteers. The volunteers are wont to say that it is not worth undertaking programs with the families if these programs favor the most dynamic members of the group, allowing some families to benefit at the expense of the whole group, breaking the bonds of solidarity within the group, and causing the departure of the strongest ones. What would a program be worth if it were to abandon the weakest? What would it mean to denounce a selective society if we were selective in our actions? In order to point toward a new society, our efforts must lead the strongest to take the side of the weakest. It is a difficult aim to achieve, and we only partially succeed. Nevertheless, that is the goal all the volunteers are striving to attain. Therein lies their strength, and their role cannot be contested.

I am tempted to say that, in the you-never-had-it-so-good society of the sixties, to speak of the family and of giving priority to the poorest meant going out of your way to seek difficulties.

We did not make up any of it. The families and their plight imposed on us the obligation to be a family movement and to make the poorest the center and the driving force of all our action. This became an absolute necessity for the volunteers, but they did not invent it. And, there was another necessity just as imperative: to reveal the families' existence and constant suffering to the outside world. This task haunted me. The volunteers understood this and shared it.

To bear witness, we had first to show what the families lived, what was forced upon them, what they suffered, and what they refused to accept. The determination to proclaim their hopes and capabilities came later. I was anxious, in the first place, to convince the authorities and public opinion of the injustice that the sociological and historical reality of their lives represented. However, I had not attended college and I was more inclined to act than to study. I tried hard to improve my reasoning and develop my knowledge, but we needed more than that. We needed evidence that was scientific. When Alwine de Vos van Steenwijk arrived, on a wintry first of January, I asked her to sort out clothes. Then, when she asked me, "What shall I do now?" I told her to go and study. She was taken aback, as André Etesse had been when I asked him to take charge of a dead man and then to preside over an association, when he had only come to deliver a package of clothes. Alwine remained pensive for a while, especially because, as she was a diplomat, I had asked her to go and study what was happening in other countries. The following day, because she was Dutch herself, I asked for her help in welcoming a Dutch journalist. Then she understood that, in order to explain things to other people and to persuade them, she had to be knowledgeable herself. This was how the Research Institute started, the first one to be started by a French association fighting extreme poverty.

Who could understand the idea of a research institute responding to the problems of a camp for homeless people?

The Institute was gradually built up, not without hardships and tears, and amid general misunderstanding. Alwine had a letterhead printed as "Social Research Bureau." She then started to do what her profession had taught her; that is, set up public relations, become known at UNESCO, and organize a study tour of the Netherlands, followed by an international symposium. We had to provide accommodations for the experts she invited to the camp at Noisy. Sessions of the working groups were held in a shack where we had to sit on piles of mattresses.

You were right to remind me that the study of poverty was not respected in France in 1960. The mention of the word "poverty" itself was not well received. At the Paris family allowances office, where they used the term "social maladjustment," the comment about our first volunteers was: "Probably yet another bunch of ladies knitting for the poor." Others said that studying poverty was a way of exploiting the families. Such slander and antagonism contributed greatly to uniting the volunteers, who were still so few at the time.

Weren't they shaken and gradually overcome by doubt?

Certainly each volunteer must have gone through periods of doubt. Some left and came back several times. But when one doubted, others stood firm. They supported each other, and so the whole group survived and grew in number.

In the early sixties, which we called the dreadful years, our determination to persevere was sustained by a particular discipline: the volunteers wrote daily observation reports and did common research. I suggested the daily reports after a visit to Great Britain. I had seen dossiers on families at the Barnardo's Home, a home for families in difficulty. My idea was to write down, each evening, what the families had told us or made us discover during the day, so that we could think over each gesture, each word or event, and make these part of ourselves. I imagined a kind of re-examination of our own lives directed entirely toward the families. Then Jean Labbens arrived. He taught us how we could transform this practice into a more systematic type of research. We decided together to make note of all the friendships, all the services rendered, and all the exchanges. At that time, about 1963, we also undertook to note down everything connected with the history of the underprivileged through the ages. In this way we began to introduce them into the history of other people and into the history of mankind.

From our viewpoint, that was a "part of the action," as we used to say. If we wanted to embark together on a long journey, it was important to give the families an opportunity to talk about their own history and the history of their parents and grandparents, and to help them to know they were honored by sharing their experience of life. We discovered this as the families told us more and more of their past. The more attentive we were, the more they revealed of their history. Reliving this history, no longer with shame but with pride in their own experience, became the highlight of the Movement's pedagogy. The volunteers working among the families had the merit of gaining their trust and of convincing them that, by this act of trust, the families were defending their own cause. Before, the families had been questioned by many people, they had

had to reply to many administrative inquiries. All this had forced them to display their own shortcomings. Investigators had shown them little respect, had violated their privacy and set traps for them in their questions: "Are you on good terms with your neighbors? Would you wish them to be rehoused with you?" The scientific community discredited itself by playing into the hands of the administration, which was bent on proving that the poor in France had no common history of their own and, besides, that they were not really poor but rather ill or feeble-minded. After these absolutely disgraceful inquiries, which left the families with an aftertaste of shame, how was it possible to engage in a new dialogue with them? It was to the credit of the families and the volunteers of that period that they set out, patiently, together, to reconstruct the families' true history.

It was an important time for the volunteer corps to become historians of the poorest. Today, some volunteers still devote their lives to writing the history of the Fourth World. No other team of volunteers has been so passionate in discovering, along with the families, a past that had never been correctly told before.

This rare passion was a source of joy to both families and volunteers. What happiness there was, indeed, in the discovery of such a history, which was imbued with the will to live, with the constant efforts to defend the dignity of the family and its right to remain united. What pride there was in telling of all the means people had to invent in order to survive and to avoid the iniquities of public services.

I have spoken of sharing the suffering, but we also shared the joy of these discoveries with a good deal of humor. What a display of imagination, what tricks were used in order to divert an investigation, to retain a benefit, or to avoid attracting the wrath of an organization. What joy in restoring bonds of friendship or kinship, in meeting a father, mother, or sister again, after having retraced a history in which they thought they had lost touch forever. During the sixties, the volunteers were full of joy and energy. They would go out on Saturday nights to dances on the banks of the River Marne. They would spend holidays in Ireland, Israel, and Africa, with hardly any money on them. Those who did not know them thought they would be dull people. They discovered that the volunteers were youthful and humorous, with plenty of drive and daring.

It seems you have given a certain solemnity or weightiness to your own approach. I note that your research was punctuated by conferences at UNESCO.

We first entered UNESCO by surprise. Who thought of organizing a congress on poverty in wealthy countries at the beginning of the sixties? Taken by surprise, UNESCO allowed itself to be persuaded; once won over, it remained a true ally. Our Movement and this specialized branch of the UN continued to fight side by side. Some years later it granted us an official consultative status.

The conferences, however, have not so much punctuated our research as they have highlighted our action. We had to make ourselves known, to convince people, and to confirm our findings by a recognized event in which other people would take a stand. Our struggle had been very hard, and we felt we should protect our findings and make them, in a way, irrefutable. After each conference—between 1963 and 1983 we organized five, either at UNESCO or with UNESCO's collaboration—we could say, "We are not the only ones to assert this; it was said at a UNESCO congress."

This may sound like a naive approach, but it has proved effective and quite realistic on the political level. It was a way of causing people and institutions with a reputation for seriousness to lend their prestige on behalf of those who had none. Academics like Jean Labbens and Christian Debuyst, institutions like UNESCO, the ILO, and UNICEF gradually threw their weight onto the scale and took risks with us. UNESCO even went so far as to denounce illiteracy in industrialized countries, basing its case mostly on data gathered by our teams at the grass-roots level.

You often mention the risk of taking a stand. Does such a risk still exist when one talks about poverty today?

It is a question of recognizing what others don't want to see; by so doing, one takes a stand. I can say that, in the course of all those years, we have come to know and influence a number of national and international administrations, one civil servant after another. In this matter, the conferences were a great help.

I can remember the first symposium, in 1961. In order to be accredited, we had to come to a compromise with the French authorities on the language we used. They did not like us to speak about poverty, and we could not accept the terms "antisocial" and "problem families," which were then used by all Western European countries. We accepted the middle-of-the-road term "maladjusted families." After this symposium, we were able to form an official working group in which public authorities took part. From then on, the idea of study was accepted and we began to call ourselves "Science and Service Teams." A number of people, however, went on describing the volunteer corps disparagingly as "scientists using the families for their own purpose." The term "poverty" really emerged only in 1970. The "war on poverty," which the U.S. government began to conduct in 1965, helped us considerably in bringing about changes in vocabulary, which then aided a shift in mentalities.

The volunteer corps was shaped, strengthened, and fortified by having to conduct so many patient battles for the recognition of the very poor as a people. Eventually, in 1968, it felt that the term "Science and Service Teams" was no longer suitable. The corps saw itself rather as a group defending human rights. It became more involved in that field as a result of sharing the lives of the poorest.

This transformation of a volunteer corps, poor among the poor, into champions of human rights seems a kind of contradiction, doesn't it?

The volunteer corps went through various stages, the first one being that of communion with the families and of sharing their suffering. At that time, incidentally, it was said that we liked misery for misery's sake; what was the use of burying oneself in the mud in such misery and disorganization? In the sixties we had extended our action to the shantytown of La Campa at La Courneuve and the emergency housing project La Cerisaie in Stains, and also to New York. We talked so much about the families' suffering that it is somewhat understandable if people thought we were preoccupied with misery for misery's sake.

Does this mean you have changed since that time?

We have moved on, I think, especially since 1968, a year in which we had an experience different from other years. Then, the majority of the working class thought, as it did in 1936, that it was the age of a new liberation and a step leading to a more just society. In the low-income housing projects, we discovered that the underprivileged were not only deprived of rights but were also excluded from the struggle for human rights. They were neither present nor represented anywhere. In 1968, we began to speak publicly of "a people" and its right to representation.

Didn't the underprivileged join the protesters in the streets?

A few younger ones did, happy to seize the opportunity of merging with the others. But most people didn't budge; they were near starvation. We came to understand then that people who had "nothing to lose" could not participate in the struggle, as could those who had something in reserve. The poorest lost the jobs they had obtained after much effort, and their allowances were not paid for some time. I saw entire areas where all the families had to live for a month on petty larceny, charity, and alms. Municipal social services, which should have given priority to supporting those families, did not grant them any money, on the pretext that they were not regularly employed workers.

Occasionally, students would go to a shantytown when they had some food left over after supplying workers on strike, and they unloaded food that often was spoiling. Once I saw the arrival of a supply of fish already going bad. It was thrown on the ground, and people were fighting for a share of it. Seldom have I had so strong a feeling of being in the depths, with people bound hand and foot to a common destitution, a common humiliation. May and June of 1968 were months of starvation in the low-income housing projects. On July 14, we organized our first Human Rights Festival, which took place at La Cerisaie in Stains. In May, we had started a students' movement called "Knowledge in the Street." For July 14, the students wrote and staged a play telling the story of the poorest during the French Revolution. Our volunteer corps was becoming indeed a defender of human rights.

Weren't you abandoning your rule of conduct of not embarking in struggles that lay outside the families' scope? They could not possibly have acquired sufficient political sense for that kind of a struggle.

Poor people's lack of political sense is a myth invented by the rich. It is probably true that our abstract way of treating political questions with reference to our doctrines cannot have any interest for men and women constantly obliged to face concrete difficulties in order to safeguard their existence and dignity. But you only have to share and analyze these real-life situations with them to become aware of the political realism of the Fourth World. It also reveals to us the degree of abstraction and lack of realism found in other social groups.

You may well ask why we had not, therefore, tackled the theme of human rights sooner; was not this lack of reference to the poorest and their absence from political life evident at a much earlier stage? It had long been true that when Fourth World children were not active in school, it did not affect the schools, and everything went on as usual. The same thing was true of trade unions and the absence of underprivileged workers in their midst. When the poorest were not present in church, that did not prevent church services from taking place. The business world did not worry about their lack of spending power. And so, there existed a state of chronic absence, an established fact that had gone on for a long time, a kind of unwritten law. We certainly had to ask ourselves where to begin. Before we could define the Movement, we had to see and live together with the poorest through the worst of times, when the poorest were ignored, abandoned, and even humiliated by the defenders of new political liberties.

This intolerable situation forced us to change course, which we did with the families' constant agreement and even encouragement. Their situation of near-starvation had forced us to collect money and food. The families were invited to form local committees to organize the distribution of money and food according to each person's needs. It was the first time in France that a truly collective responsibility was being taken on in the poorest housing projects. The debate about giving priority to the poorest, to the hungriest, and to the most neglected children became a central one and was brought to public attention. The families carried out their task very honorably during those weeks, in all the places we were able to visit. In the process, they became more aware of their existence as a people. Those who had known us for a long time found it quite natural that we extend our action to other places previously unknown to us. They exchanged grievances with one another. We had known for years that our mission was to bring to light a people, to enable it to leave its mark on history and to assume its role vis-à-vis its fellow citizens. May and June of 1968 constituted a climax that allowed us to translate those aims into action for human rights. This strengthened the volunteer corps as it discovered a new atmosphere, new tools, and a new strategy.

The volunteer corps also acquired something altogether original, insofar as from then on it could not allow human rights to be systematically reduced solely to civil and political rights. The Fourth World was teaching us that such a limitation, which is still prevalent, is totally artificial. To speak of political freedom without taking into account economic, social, and cultural rights may be valid for people who are comfortably well off, but not for the working class and still less for the poorest. Since 1968, the Fourth World Movement has denounced the restrictive nature of human rights campaigns that reduce these to political rights only.

By so doing, you were on the road to politicization. Were you then able to weigh the dangers of such a position—in particular, that of imposing certain political choices on the poor?

I do not know where the boundary between political activity and sectarian politics lies exactly. The Movement and the volunteer corps did not acquire their political dimension in 1968. They had it from the beginning, otherwise they would not have upset people so much and they would have not been the object of so much slander. From 1968 on, the volunteer corps became unreservedly engaged in political action and protest. In 1968, it followed in the steps of Dufourny de Villiers who had compiled the "Cahiers de Doléances" for the General Assembly of the Three Orders at the time of the French Revolution. Similar "Grievances Notebooks" were written from housing projects in all parts of France, and we published them in book form under the title *Un Peuple Parle* (A People Speaks). From then on, the Movement was present in every local, national, and European electoral campaign. But the question is probably not how far we can go in our political action, but in what way we can remain unfailingly rooted in the hope of the very poor as a people. How can we be assured we will stay at the right level, that of their essential aspirations? What can prevent us from getting involved in petty struggles and partisan politics and, consequently, in political domination over the poorest?

What is your answer to these questions today? What assurances does the volunteer corps give itself?

I don't know whether permanent solutions exist. We could say that the families themselves are the guarantee, but even that is not certain. I told you before that they don't feel comfortable in the existing structures. They are unable to truly confront these structures, since the structures continue to work without them. Therefore they are unable to suggest immediately what structural and political changes they would benefit from.

The same inability affects society at large, because it does not experiment with its structures in relation to the poorest. To deal with their situation, our society offers individual interventions; that is, someone, on his or her own initiative, tries to improve the situation. Thus, the underprivileged, although absent from institutions, are not absent from other peoples' lives. A person will reject another person less readily than structures do. A teacher, a social worker, or a priest will intervene, for better or worse incidentally, and sometimes by taking charge of the children. We could speak here of a deep-rooted attraction of people for people. A human being can never completely lose interest in another flesh-and-blood human being. This is probably the reason why so many persons intervene in the lives and in the future of the families. They don't go far enough; they don't always act when they should; but at least they intervene. This is because human beings cannot accept the disorder created by others or the fact that they cannot understand others. How often have I heard people declare, "I know these families perfectly well. I know everything about them." In fact, the social workers or nuns who say that do not know the families, but how could they admit it? It would amount to disowning a part of humanity in themselves. I am convinced that most cases of tactless behavior and of coercive measures result from this impossibility of admitting that we do not understand the humanity of the other person. If they do not behave as we do, something must be missing in their humanity. For this reason we feel a personal duty to help them back to the straight path.

The absence of adequate structures does not, therefore, mean the absence of people involved in the life of the families. They, themselves, are constantly looking for other people. This shows us that every human being needs other people as a complement, and this is not only natural but also essential to his or her own life. The poorest, unable to have recourse to anonymous and impersonal structures, are telling us, perhaps more clearly than others, that one way or another a human being always hopes to reach other human beings. This is why I am less and less able to understand why the Church is not more present in the world of the poor. The poor have such a great need to meet priests and nuns in flesh and blood, committed Christians and catechists, people they can circumvent, whom they can outsmart if need be, and whom they can use as go-betweens. The exclusion of any direct relationship in the practice of charity was a major mistake. I am speaking here of charity in terms of aid, of an entirely natural relationship of assistance, which is as necessary for the survival of the poorest as for that of the givers. By giving up this personal relationship in mutual aid, the Church has given up the person-to-person response to real-life situations. Instead of replacing it with new personal commitments, the Church has created organized aid; that is, a structure, which is much worse than the old personal relationships. It is true that these were not the best possible ones, but they entailed personal contact, which is still needed by underprivileged families. The Church needs these, too, if it wants to learn how to give these families a privileged place in its human structures.

I want to come back to these questions of structures and of the dangers of politicization for the Fourth World volunteer corps. If the volunteers remain personally attached to the families, and if they continue to want to learn from them day after day, they will necessarily always be led back to this hand-to-hand struggle, which will prevent them from taking refuge in theories that advocate changing structures just for the sake of it. I am not saying volunteers are proof against this temptation. Anybody and everybody is always ready to flee from extreme poverty. We can live in a low-income neighborhood and manage not to be at the mercy of the people. Sometimes, just by organizing the life of our own family, our free time, our vacations, or our sabbatical year, we can avoid being at their mercy. Then we no longer hear a people's voice; we are no longer at their mercy, and hearing them ceases to be a vital necessity for us.

If even the fact of living among the families is not a sufficient guarantee of a person-to-person relationship, aren't you worried about the future?

Yes, I am very worried; and yet I have confidence. If there is a guarantee, it can only be the volunteer corps. They have to be a guarantee for each other. I believe this is something the volunteers learn during their annual meetings. All those who have been engaged in the volunteer corps for more than five years, and who agree to take on responsibilities toward this corps as a whole, meet every summer. They reflect together, not on what they have to do but on what they are and what they have to be. Taking part in those annual meetings means a personal commitment to guarantee that the volunteer corps as a whole remains faithful to the poorest. And only the volunteer corps as a whole can guarantee the faithfulness, the sincerity, and the human quality of each volunteer. For their part, the families require these same qualities but they cannot guarantee them.

All this presupposes an alert and open mind at all times, much humility, self-control, and an absence of false pride. In addition to annual meetings, we have introduced what we call "planning and evaluation" sessions. The self-imposed discipline of formulating precise objectives, of "planning from the hopes of the families," of submitting oneself to evaluate the results of one's efforts—all this helps the volunteer corps to guard against its own frailty. Its main merit may lie in its not being sure of itself.

It remains to be seen if the volunteer corps, whose wish is to contribute to the liberation of the underprivileged, is prepared to become unnecessary and to work for its own disappearance.

We kept saying this all through the first years: One day the people will be free and will no longer need us. We may have been mistaken in thinking that freedom lay at the end of the road. In fact, the underprivileged wherever they are, and every single family among them, must be independent from the start. From the very beginning the families and the volunteer corps enter into a communal life where freedom should be ensured—not only the freedom of individual families or places but also the freedom of other families and groups as yet unknown to us. I told you that every poor person hides a poorer one. Behind the housing projects of France, were hidden those of Germany and Britain. Behind these, hide those with the worst reputation and conditions: the encampments of West Africa.

When we went to the United States, and then to Latin America, Africa, and the Far East, some criticized us for dissipating our efforts. They were wrong. It was high time for us to broaden the European families' horizon and make them aware of the urge to stand by the poorest families in the Ivory Coast and the Upper Volta.[14] It was their right. The poorest becoming the apostles of humanity—this cannot remain just an idea; it has to be translated into reality. The families from underprivileged housing projects in Versailles and Créteil and from the most disadvantaged neighborhoods in Glasgow and Rotterdam, have the absolute right to be in the front line of the wider struggle for a world without exclusion.

When I went to India in 1965, families from the camp at Noisy who wore secondhand clothes collected food and clothing for the poor in Bombay. A moment ago, you mentioned the danger of politicization. It is always a real one. A volunteer corps such as ours always runs the risk of trapping itself in the present moment. But the solution does not lie in remaining outside partisan politics. One must go beyond that. When the poorest and we together have succeeded in placing ourselves at the level of building the world, they themselves will choose their local community or national society. In fact, this is the command: "Put out into the deep and let down your nets for a catch." That is: Let us not stop within the limits of the society in which we live, but let us go out into the whole world.

10.

"Priority Given to the Poorest": What Does It Mean?

Gilles Anouil: The word "movement" is very important to you. You said, "I started an association with the first allies, and the volunteer corps pushed me to start a Movement." What is the difference?

Father Joseph Wresinski: The difference lies in the concept of a movement. An association can set up its by-laws, define its role and its way of working. This does not mean that it stops there and becomes out-of-date or cumbersome, but it is true that an association pays the price of its security through a certain inability to keep up-to-date. It may be innovative initially, but has a difficult time remaining so. In my mind, a movement sets itself up in order to be able to pull up its tent and move on. A movement is designed to hold the road equipped only with conviction, experience, and knowledge.

The volunteer corps, dedicated to extending human rights to the poorest, wanted to make the existence of a people possible by being its mirror and its voice. We didn't yet know who these families were or where they wanted to go. This still remains true. We say that society, especially the working world, should recognize the Fourth World and make it the main cause for their struggles. The volunteer corps must pursue this objective by constantly being ready to cross borders. On either side of the border there are people, and to these people we must be bound. The volunteer corps has to enter the history and the way of thinking of flesh-and-blood human beings. On either side, there is no way of dictating choices; we have to be convincing. For this to happen, our ways of working and our language must be intelligible, adapted to the time and place. Being a volunteer in Amsterdam or New York is not quite the same as being a volunteer in the Paris area. In Dakar or Ouagadougou, it will be even more different. It will differ in all but the essentials: the desire to discover the poorest, to walk alongside them, and to discover how they can be a focal point for people around them. When planning a program in the Movement, we foresee more questions than answers. How shall we go about enabling a population to reveal its aspirations as regards work and health? How shall we go about discovering the unexpected?

The Movement is a search, not an answer. It is a permanent invitation to collaborate in that search. It is a search for the poorest and for those around them, as well as a search for our own identity as a Movement. What does it mean to be an interdenominational movement where all ideologies are comfortable with each other? What will this Movement be tomorrow?

Does this mean that you have no structures? You are reproached by some for being unorganized.

Some people expect us to have traditional structures, a hierarchy, an infrastructure, and the controls that you would usually find elsewhere. They are surprised to hear that at the Movement's general secretariat we don't know what is happening in such and such a local project. Is the Movement disorganized? The situation is all the more disconcerting because, at certain times, this same general secretariat will intervene in what seems to be a mere detail in a local project.

This at times surprises even our own allies. It is not disorder, but a different type of order, based on other priorities. It is an order that safeguards essentials without burdening ourselves with unnecessary luggage that would weigh us down. What is essential is priority for the poorest—the absolute necessity of meeting them, of knowing them, of basing all our efforts on them and their need for a corps of volunteers totally at their service. We should not deviate from these points in the slightest. No structure or bureaucracy seems to be able to ensure this. This is clear when one looks at the history of Western society and the history of the Church. Innumerable institutions have been set up to benefit the poor throughout the ages. How many of them have remained faithful? They have become attached to certain people, have contributed to their development and have advanced with them. The fact that they were conceived and founded for the poor did not stop them from moving on with people who were no longer poor. The Movement does not presume it is capable of doing better. However, we would like to learn a lesson from the experience of others and give ourselves some guarantees. Therefore, we try to guarantee that we keep to the essentials through long-term training, annual meetings for full-fledged volunteers, and planning and evaluation sessions which bring all the full-time workers together and foster mutual questioning. Together they plan, develop, and modify the lines of action. The allies accept these lines because they trust the volunteers, who are closer to the families than they are. They believe in the sincerity of the volunteers, who are always trying to decipher the message of a people so they can adjust to it. Without that type of trust, they cannot be allies.

All this implies not the absence of a hierarchy but a different hierarchy. First are the poorest and those who have devoted themselves to live precisely from the perspective of the poorest. Professional hierarchies do not apply to us; the most committed and those who have been formed by extreme poverty for the longest time lead the struggle.

Doesn't that prevent your programs from being supported by public authorities? How would they accept that commitment has more weight than professional competence?

I wasn't talking about professional competence but about professional hierarchy. Most often, professional training and hierarchies have been developed without consideration for the poorest; therefore, they do not guarantee competency in helping the poor. Without a specific commitment to or training in the Fourth World, teachers, doctors, and social workers are not competent. The authorities and the professionals usually agree on the fact that training is necessary but not always on the fact that commitment is necessary.

Besides, nothing hinders public support for our programs. We try to maintain the necessary rigor in our own administration without obstructing the field of action. A good management is indispensable in order to collaborate with public services and also to be accountable to all those who support us. However, one of the worst dangers threatening the Movement is that of "management." Management simplifies problems and their solutions. The liberation of people is complex and does not follow a linear progression. It takes two steps forward, and one step backward or sideways. Because we have always tried to foresee the steps backward or sideways, we have been criticized for being complicated. We, ourselves, have to make sure that our action does not become a system or a methodology. In the meantime we do not shun dossiers, filing systems, or computer technology. But we make the same demands on them as we make on ourselves: they must contribute in the most direct way possible toward changing the life of the poorest; they must constantly be adapted toward this end.

Some people do say of you that every time they go to see you, something has changed. They also complain about the frequent transfer of volunteers.

The transfers aren't frequent enough. Some volunteers remain attached to the same place for too long a time. It is difficult to convince them they have to go.

I told you about the choices offered by extreme poverty. Either we reject those who bear it, or we take on their suffering. The third option is not to notice it any more. Because we so immerse ourselves in it, we can come to a point where we no longer perceive its odor or recognize how destitution wears a person out. To understand poverty, you sometimes have to withdraw from it. To strengthen our love, we have to maintain some distance. People who do not know how to keep their distance end up living in a kind of routine. They no longer miss the other person, nor do they recognize in what ways that person has enriched their lives.

Permanent members of the Movement are those who refuse to get into a routine that would eventually lead to marginalization and pauperization. That is contrary to what the poorest expect from us. They can become fully themselves and respectful of us only if we are fully ourselves on an intellectual and spiritual level. If the Fourth World were not a permanent occasion for intellectual and spiritual enrichment for us, then the poverty we live in would be just mimicry—an insult to the poor in that we would take on their material condition as showy rags, as a ceremonial costume.

We need to be simultaneously in proximity to extreme poverty and distant from it. Proximity, because the poorest are our common concern and our raison d'être. Distance, because they must be able to help us progress constantly in our own lives. The great opportunity the Movement offers is that its cause is, at one and the same time, individuals who suffer and a people who are on the move, forcing us to move with them.

The fact that they are individuals prevents us from making the people into a reason, an excuse, or an alibi for a struggle. Individuals force us to live at their rhythm and to make their heartbeats, their hopes, and their thoughts our own. The fact that they are also a people forces us to stay as we are—men and women to whom the poor can say, "You can do all you want, but you will never be able to understand because you haven't experienced what we are going through." If they couldn't say that to us, we wouldn't be forced to give them the right to speak. The poorest have the right to control and to correct; they can exercise this right only if they and we each stay in our proper place. So as not to lose sight of either our place or theirs, each one of us must accept changes in assignment, times of retreat for writing, or projects far from the field that aim to influence public opinion or public officials.

How do volunteers who go away remain close to the realities? How are the allies nurtured by these realities?

We have a certain way of choosing themes of interest. Teams in the field are regularly asked questions such as, "What is the families' experience with school?" or, "What do they want in regard to work?" Thus the teams are kept alert; they know they are witnesses for the Movement of what the families live and hope. The other volunteers and allies then have the task of transmitting what has been witnessed. However, we cannot transmit what we have not really taken in; we have to take time to reflect and internalize real experiences if we are to convince other people. Otherwise, very soon, we will lead another struggle, and it will be our own. Then the poor would be merely the objects of our combat; they would no longer be combatants or masters of their own cause.

I hear you say that the Movement as a whole is in a state of research, and this research is different from a scientific study. However, since 1960, you have been speaking of scientific research. What is its role? Isn't it to reveal the reality of extreme poverty?

Everything depends on the objectives of the research. Basically, scientific research always runs the risk of treating a population group purely as people to be studied. Scientists want to be the only ones to determine the course research will take, submitting only to scientific rigor and curiosity. They seem to establish a healthy distance with regard to the poor, but it is that of a voyeur rather than someone entirely open to an encounter. Science as the world knows it has chosen itself as its own master and cannot serve another at the same time. Among the volunteers, those who engage in research try to discover for themselves the meaning of "the poor as our masters." They make an intense effort to listen to the families. The research involves all the volunteers. The scientists provide the capacity for analysis and synthesis, but they do not claim to collect or interpret the data. They offer the security of well-structured and well-informed minds; and they are our shields against intellectual prejudices and misuses. In fact, in the Movement, scientists are similar to managers and other professionals—they have to reinvent a profession that was set up without a sound knowledge of the poorest. Our scientists are innovators in their field.

You spoke of the danger of structures as crippling, of management as over-simplifying, and of science as subjecting the poor. What other dangers do you see?

There is an activism that all of us can fall prey to. Doing things reassures and satisfies us: if we don't succeed today, we will succeed tomorrow. We run the risk of losing sight of the frailty of the people we work with and of the obstacles they encounter. We no longer notice their resistance; we are no longer careful to make sure they are an integral part of our action; the poor become simply the objects of our success. In a struggle for liberation, too often we think we are liberating others, whereas we are liberating ourselves. The point is not to know who is liberated, but whether the poorest are liberated with us.

For this reason, the main virtue of volunteers in a poor area should be the ability to remain silent. They must also let other volunteers question them: To what type of liberation does your action lead? Can the families recognize that they are members of a community that is willing to fight for itself? Saint Vincent de Paul said, "We must be pardoned for what we give to the poor." I would add that we have to be pardoned for our liberation struggles, which so often oppress them. There is also a danger of volunteers in the field forgetting that other volunteers severely miss being with the families. Those volunteers, who are the backup team essential to the struggle, accept being a support and a homeland to the others. They carry on an assignment without having the security given by daily contacts and struggle together in the field. They cannot say they fight for such and such a poor neighborhood and experience its difficulties.

It seems to me that the Movement brings together a maximum number of conflicting situations; for example, between religious denominations or ideologies, between allies and volunteers, between professions, between those in the field and those in offices. Have you known any attempts to form a splinter group? It seems inevitable.

What we are carrying together is very special and very strong. It is true that poverty itself is a conflict that can lead us to rise up against one another according to our ideological or political outlook. However, the hope or the determination to give priority to the poorest can unite us. That is the strength of the Movement. The primacy of the poorest pulls us away from all corporate and sector-based struggles in order to project us onto a higher level. It makes us live at the grass-roots in the most squalid poverty, and it compels us to place ourselves at heights we had not contemplated. This creates unity among us. We are far from being a religious community, and we are not a commune either. The volunteers are more like comrades-in-arms, bonded by their commitment, with all its implications of freedom and vigor of expression.

We have not known any splintering. Many people have created movements or associations inspired by their experiences with us. This was never done in opposition to us. It is, in fact, difficult to declare that one is, in good faith, opposed to the Movement, which is simply a permanent offer one can accept or refuse. It is difficult to say that you are against the liberation of the poor or that a particular ideology or strategy is imposed on you. We have no dogma, no common program.

Aren't you responsible for this unity? Aren't you like the geometric axis, the one who defuses conflicts?

I'm not exactly sure of my role, but I think it is more complex. The Movement remains essentially a place of uncontrolled freedom, not burdened by the prestige of its founder. Few organizations offer such freedom to their members. Neither do our members have to pay tribute to a mythical founder. There is nothing mythical about me, and they don't need to take care of my image. I make my own preserves,[15] I attend meetings of the Economic and Social Council, I attend meetings of the families, I celebrate Mass, and I read reports. I am as free as they are, and I am in no way an important person.

You are, however, a point of reference.

I am a point of reference only because of my intuitions and my sensitivity toward to the Fourth World. People trust me, and I think they identify me with the Fourth World, with all the good and bad luck it brings. They know that I accept everything—everything, that is, except seeing the families hurt. In return they accept from me more than they would from someone else. I have no diplomas, nor am I brilliant or prestigious. But they really think I carry the conscience of a people, not as a personal wealth or a right that couldn't be transmitted or as something inherited by or designated for me. It is simply because history decreed that someone be that conscience.

I told you that, among us, there is no checking up on people, no power structure, and no image to live up to. The Movement may very well go in a direction I would not have chosen. But everyone knows that, if the Movement were to betray the families, I would leave and start another Movement. My mission is for people, not for an organization. And it is the very realization of having such a mission, beyond other missions, that creates the unity of Fourth World.

You say: if the Movement were to betray the families. By this, you probably mean: if it no longer served as their spokesperson. This reminds me of political parties that claim to personify a population group; for example, the socialist and the communist parties. They could go so far as to say that they personify the proletariat and the underprivileged, and I think that in some countries they do say this. Where is the difference with the Movement?

These political parties are very sincere in their attachment to a people. But they have drawn assumptions from this attachment, which the people themselves can no longer question. They claim to hold a truth or a correct interpretation about the people. This is a risk for all those who opt to fight for a specific population group. If they choose it, they must persevere to the end with its liberation, even if it involves the risk of being rejected by the people once they have been liberated. They must accept the loss of their own freedom and help the population acquire the audacity to refute them. Otherwise they risk raising false hopes in the people and, sooner or later, exploiting them. Defenseless people are necessarily at the mercy of our acts of generosity. If these acts do not grow into true acts of liberation, we are halted halfway, and we settle into an idea rather than continue to let ourselves be challenged by people. The people thus become a pretext and objects rather than subjects.

The advantage of the Movement is to have no preconceived ideas to which the people might become subjected. It never stops pooling its discoveries and asking itself questions. It does not pretend to have the answer or to have the last word about the very poor as a people. The volunteer corps wants only to be a constant interpreter, encouraging this people through permanent questioning to develop its ideas and aspirations in its own chosen way. If the Movement were to set up an "underprivileged truth," it would become like a cancer in the flesh of the poorest. The Movement would then be superfluous.

I told you that the basic structures of the Movement are training, the volunteer corps meetings, and planning sessions. These are structures that allow questioning, the pooling of ideas, and the deepening of knowledge. You will not find there any program whose main theme is not the people. The Movement and its commitments always come second. No ideology or vision of society overrides the people. Liberation has no pre-established form; it is a continuing process that has to be examined in light of the current thinking and the situation of a people on the move. This is somewhat like the image of Plato's shadow: The light is behind, in the knowledge of what has gone before, and the shadow is in front, in what a people is going to teach us today and tomorrow. It is the process of a permanent cultural revolution.

Have you any concrete examples of this process dictated by the aspirations of a people?

I told you about May 1968, when the families showed they could not understand being kept apart from what gave hope to an entire society. Some underprivileged workers were so hurt by this that they pretended to be on strike, whereas they had been out of work for a longer time. This forced us to take up the question of representation and participation as part of a basic right. But the families also led us to take positions in other fields—in the field of instruction and knowledge, for example. I could talk to you about knowledge. The families had always suffered because of their lack of knowledge, and we set up places of learning with them. But this was done at the local level by some of our teams individually. In the seventies, material living conditions improved temporarily for poor people in almost all European Community countries. Then, families here and there gave us signs that the time had come for setting up a real national and international campaign for knowledge. Thus we launched our 1977 campaign: "In ten years' time there will not be a single illiterate or unemployed person in our communities. Those who know will teach those who don't." Fourth World people wanted this and, on the whole, they were ready to take on this ideal. Earlier, we could have launched such a challenge ourselves, and the people would probably have pretended to follow without really putting their heart in it. And also, if we had not paid enough attention to the signs they gave us then, we would have missed the right moment. But, fortunately, we were receptive and attentive to such signs in the various areas at that time.

The sessions you hold so regularly for the volunteer corps seem to be a sort of healthy discipline for the Movement.

The sessions grew out of the simple meetings we held right from the very first years. As you know, the urge to understand a people in order to proclaim their existence and to obtain for them the means to express themselves, is what led to the founding of the Movement. The sessions, during which we question one another, are like the "breathing" of the volunteer corps. The meetings remain true person-to-person encounters. They are "horizontal" relations, designed for the progress of each one. They prevent the Movement from closing in on itself like a caste or from becoming exclusive. The number of volunteers attending them increased gradually. Keep in mind that about a hundred volunteers attend the volunteer corps meetings and some two hundred the planning sessions, and that they represent fourteen nationalities and all ages.

Since the sixties, the volunteer corps has also been running international work camps each summer, where young people come with their questions and ideas. For the volunteers, the work camps are much more a responsibility than a help, despite the fact that the participants do long days of manual work. But the volunteer corps is revitalized through them, by being exposed to the currents of opinion prevailing among each new generation.

These young people probably ask you the same question I'm going to ask: Between reform and revolution, which do you choose?

Is that the right question? The poorest have seen so many reforms and revolutions that have brought them nothing. They are both ways of dealing the cards differently to those already playing. In order to make room for new players, dealing the cards differently is not enough; the rules of the game have to be changed. The Movement is often reproached for not "playing the game."

It doesn't join the game of recognized partners. This is true, since it brings a new player to the card table. And this is equally inconvenient for all.

How can we choose our position in the debate between reformists and revolutionaries? Our duty is to ask everyone: Where are the poorest? In this respect, the Movement is a lone watchman in the night. By asking everyone the question about the poorest, the Movement affirms its conviction that everyone has to contribute to the invention of new rules. Here are two principles that are not fashionable at the moment: to believe in the fragility of our systems and ideologies, and to accept the need to examine all our undertakings in view of the excluded. This is not a new value in our societies, but they have not applied it. To say that all our fellow citizens, all the political parties and trade unions, all our institutions and churches must contribute to the search for and the introduction of the poorest into their lives is not new either. But this effort to be united around the excluded is not one of the rules of the game in the modern world.

Doesn't the Movement make the search for the poorest its own?

The Movement personifies an attempt at that search, in which reformers and revolutionaries must equally participate, thus putting their convictions to the test. This constantly challenges anything that does not give priority to the Fourth World. The Movement makes the Fourth World a witness to the exclusiveness of our societies and of our struggles to transform them. The Movement does not wish to usurp responsibility from individuals. Each person has to make this effort. Day by day, from the families, we try to decipher guidelines for a school, for professional training, and for a system of guaranteed income corresponding to their hopes. Every social class and social circle has its own experts. To a certain extent, the volunteers attempt to be experts for the Fourth World, and this costs them considerable effort day and night. However, nothing we do or try to be can replace the efforts that should be made by others.

Some people try to divert the volunteer corps from its true masters. A minister, a government, or a specialized UN agency will ask us to spell out our recommendations: "What precise changes are needed in the social security system? What are the details of a good program against illiteracy? What exactly should be done for children's health?" Public authorities often ask for painstaking answers, with little or no compensation or commitment on their part and sometimes without any payment. Too often, the volunteer gets caught in the trap through fear that otherwise things won't change for the families. We might get involved where we don't have to, in order to avoid accusations of remaining vague and failing to spell out concrete steps. This is a false reproach, but it is often used as an excuse for not getting involved: "How do you expect me to take the initiative if you don't give me a detailed procedure?"

By too often accepting that kind of pressure to facilitate change, the volunteer corps has sometimes missed opportunities to develop an idea or solution with the families. At one point, a public service put much pressure on the volunteers to become involved in a given area: "Take care of the young people; see to the welfare of newborn babies." And this would have happened even before people in the community had the time to get to know the team of volunteers, to see with whom they were dealing. The intention of the public authorities may be genuine and often they sincerely want to help us. But, as a director of the Ministry for Cooperation said when he observed a Fourth World program in Upper Volta,[16] "The state cannot finance preparatory stages to development." And this is a great shame, because by not giving the time and the means of preparation to the people concerned, one can act much too casually, intervening in the life of a population while totally ignoring their feelings, unable to see their eventual reactions. This shows a deep lack of respect, as if those who intervene don't even imagine that thoughts and feeling exist. They don't realize it is important for a group to freely decide whether to be involved in a program, to influence its course, to oppose it or to refuse it. Merely thinking about this would in itself be a revolution.

When the volunteer corps decides to present a detailed dossier or even to undertake a program at the request of a local or national authority, one can reproach it for collaborating with the government and being used as an alibi. This is not always entirely false, but that is not the main point. The truth is, whether they are reformist or revolutionary, all the current authorities are equally afraid of changing the rules of the game in favor of the Fourth World.

What kinds of changes are the most feared?

The point is not to prioritize specific minor changes; it is to cease to see people through the lens of their problems, one by one. The change required is to fully assume the dignity of the poor, to take their thinking as a reference point for all policies, and their hope as a reference point for all action. This type of revolution in the way of thinking and in the way of looking at people is unsettling for all of us. To encounter the same question at every moment and every bend in the road: "What have you done unto me?" destroys any intellectual and material security. We would have to build security of another nature. This is the reversal of priorities the Movement is talking about.

Indeed, it is truly a reversal in mentality and practice—and is consequently a revolution.

Yes, and we are reproached with this also: either of being vague and not demanding enough, or of demanding too much. In fact, we are asking the national and international community to experiment with new practices and to give signs of their determination not to give up. It is true that we ask for a global approach with the poorest; that is, not to start with financial security without thinking of professional training, for example, and not to undertake the security of employment without planning for that of housing.

It is difficult to make people understand that, as a consequence, all citizens will benefit. In the sixties, at a time of full employment, we were issuing strong warnings: "If you leave people without any possibility of being useful, you are leaving a worm in the fruit, and tomorrow the fruit will be rotten." Today this is being confirmed by the fact that society accepts unemployment on a vast scale. Today we discover that full employment was not an absolute right demanded by our societies, but solely the outcome of an economic situation. Similarly, in all our industrialized societies, some children leave school practically illiterate, thus endangering all children. We are already a society that allows illiteracy. Tomorrow, when the illiterate are those who cannot master electronics, hundreds of thousands of our fellow citizens will be unable to communicate through computer technology. This won't make us indignant either.

A society that is allowed to leave one single person without work, without education, without housing, without political participation, without prayer or knowledge of God, will deprive others in the future. It is a society, a school, and a church without foundations. While some children and adults are able to escape from the bottom—the rich will usually succeed in keeping up with changes—the little people, the individuals, and families without many reserves, will fall into the abyss. This is why we should do away with corporate and partial struggles, in order to reverse priorities. By making the most disadvantaged the starting point of our thoughts and the driving force of our action, we are building a community in which life is good to all. The underprivileged raise the alarm on today's scandal; they also predict and announce the scandal of tomorrow.

This is a hidden scandal. You, yourself, denounce our ignorance. How many French people know the number of their fellow citizens who have remained illiterate?

I asked whether that ignorance is an excuse. Is it admissible? In a society where a person cannot live without writing, is it acceptable not to be on the lookout for those who are poorly served and forgotten by school? Is a society acceptable if it does not keep watch in the night?

Our country does not know the number of families who sleep in the open, wandering from one shelter to another. It keeps an account of all its housing without wanting to know exactly who lives in it. Homeless families are omitted from the count. The country has not asked its statistical services or its public authorities to account for the most essential thing: the condition of the poorest. The country knows what it wants to know, and its leaders don't answer questions that aren't put to them.

What are we to make in all this of the beatitudes? Or of the call in Matthew's gospel: "I was homeless and you gave me shelter."[17]? This is not only a moral imperative but a political one. Do you think that Jesus Christ is homeless only in other countries? He is homeless on our doorstep, and he asks us whether housing is a matter of having an income and the ability to be a good neighbor, or whether the very existence of a family justifies its right to housing.

Therefore, the Lord would reverse all the rights to which we attach a minimum of duties?

Jesus Christ does not release us from our duties. He said, "I was hungry and you fed me; I was lost and you found me." One day I spoke about housing to the private secretary of a minister. He replied that to guarantee housing regardless of the merits and capabilities of a family was to question the very concept of lodging and all the structures of French housing. The same type of reply was given to me at the Ministry of National Education when I asked for the introduction of computers in special classes, which are the last chance for very poor children within the French educational system. I was asked, "Do you think that's all our Ministry of National Education has to do?" Yes, as a matter of fact, I do. Many problems would be solved if they did only this: laid a basis for French education. Not any old minimum standard, but a basis that would serve as a true impetus for the poorest. I hear the same argument, "That's not all we have to do," in all the ministries, and I persist in thinking their most important task is just that.

They will tell you it will be too expensive.

They might also tell me it has been tried in vain in the former Soviet Union or Hungary. In fact we don't know. The notion of high cost stems from our inability to imagine offering to the poor what we would not offer to the rich. To introduce computers in special classes represents a modest expense. Obviously the cost will be higher if we feel we have to install them, perhaps first of all, in the other branches of the educational system. Most of us believe this. The idea of the priority of the poorest is not familiar to us; it appears incompatible with any notion of political and economic efficiency.

As for universal housing in the former Soviet Union or equal wages in Hungary, they have not lasted and they were never entirely dissociated from the idea of merit. In any case, it was not a question of privileging the poorest but of giving to everyone equally. One is the opposite of the other. We do not know of any society where giving priority to the poorest has been tried. There is no model for it. Nor is there a model for the Kingdom of God. We shall have to advance step by step, groping our way along.

All this does not answer your question: reform or revolution.

You propose that we advance step by step but with a 180 degree change of direction.

I am thinking of a woman who has eight children. She is having a terrible time trying to obtain her family allowances, decent housing, and free school meals for the children. Her partner does not work, and she is not legally married to him. At the city office, people say of her, "You really have to be good-for-nothing and completely irresponsible to have eight children. Who does she think she is? She comes here all the time, asking for help."

Everywhere she goes this mother creates a whirlwind; she is a real hindrance. She perplexes welfare and housing management workers. With her large family and no resources, this woman presents a basic problem to society and its way of seeing human beings. She is the test of our sincerity about human rights. Her partner is illiterate and has been beaten down by life; he does not know how to assume his responsibilities toward a job. He has never been integrated into the working world and has not assimilated its rigor and logic. Shall we give him some work and on-the-job training because we think he will be worthwhile, or because he has the right to the dignity of being useful? Or shall we tell him, as I like repeating, "You exist, we exist; we are bonded by the same destiny, which is our common opportunity."

As it is, the institutions will find an excuse for giving him nothing except some meager aid through social welfare. The family will continue to be treated as inferior from every point of view. For whom, then, are human rights intended and for whom is there liberation? You have asked me questions about the Movement. As long as it keeps the poorest as an essential reference point, as long as its only raison d'être is a people standing upright and in a state of hope, we shall be able to trust this Movement. As long as the poorest people can say to our Movement, "What you are saying is just what I think and could not manage to say," it will be a path for the liberation of the poorest.

11.

The Theology of Liberation

Gilles Anouil: You speak of the liberation of the poor. This is a theme discussed in the Church, where we are currently witnessing a lively debate on liberation theology. What is your position on this matter? Let me quote a few words of Monsignor Proaño, a bishop in Ecuador. You can tell me what you think.

> *In Latin America, we are all more or less in a state of slavery, in our mental structures and in the mechanisms of our social structures. Christ did not come simply to liberate us as individuals but also collectively. Capitalism is a state of sin, as was stated in Medellín in 1968. The gospel has to be embodied in everyday reality, otherwise we become accomplices in the established social injustice. Liberation theology is not simply carried out by intellectuals but by the poor who have a marvelous intuition for picking up the essential part of the Christian message and of whom it is true to say that the poor evangelize us.*

Father Joseph Wresinski: How can one not be in agreement with a liberation that is both spiritual and social? In Latin America, it seems to me, however, that there is still a great deal of confusion.

The Popes have said that the Church is implacable as regards injustice. The Church rises up with persistence and without compromise against low salaries, homelessness of families, and non-achievement of children in the education system. The duty of the Church is to reject systems that oppress, that make the poorest inferiors for life without any hope of a better existence. We are all in agreement on this point, and I understand the protest of Christians in Latin America, the priests who are shocked and outraged at the acts of injustice perpetrated against the poor. Meanwhile, disagreements can arise about the way to oppose the system. The Church cannot tolerate any attack on another person, be he rich or poor. In the eyes of the Church, to attack the rich also means to attack the poor. If we accustom the poor to despise the rich, we change the masters by creating new slaves.

The words of Christ, "The first will be last," are at the same time an affirmation and a prophecy. Jesus Christ has accomplished the change and, one day, people will share places and responsibilities differently. But the Lord has never said that the rich should be humiliated or oppressed in their turn. For Christians, the liberation of the poor is certainly a struggle, but it cannot be just any type of struggle.

More fundamentally, whoever speaks of theology speaks of the knowledge of God and human beings. It is impossible to separate one from the other, since the covenant between them is definitive. A theology of liberation must therefore examine the link between human freedom and God's freedom. To understand the free person, one has to know who the free God is. When I went to Latin America, I kept asking the same question: The liberation of which person, in relation to which God? I never received a reply.

It seems that the people they told me about were always those who still had a bite to eat.[17] In a way they could afford to speak lightly of God, the Church, and society; they could always resurface because they had kept something in reserve. I could see, on one side, entire neighborhoods of men, women, and children who were immersed in extreme cultural, spiritual, and economic underdevelopment. And on the other side, there were those people, often well-read, with an acute political awareness. I ended up doubting whether the latter were really, as they claimed to be, the conscience of the poorest.

John Paul II says that the Church is the conscience of all consciences. I like this concept very much. It is especially applicable to the commitment of Christians in the struggle for liberation. Someone always pays for this liberation. Is it because I have known extreme poverty and been in close contact with it all my life? When faced with this type of approach by educated people, I always feel a bit threatened and tend to react self-defensively: Aren't they forgetting to look for and question the poorest? And in this matter of conscience, whose conscience is it?

160 The Poor Are the Church

I am afraid there are many misunderstandings on this point. Nothing guarantees that the proposed liberation represents an opportunity for the poorest. Have the poorest been understood through a long relationship and a profound communion of life and destiny? Have the projects really been developed together with them? In my opinion, these projects are ahead of the poor, as projects always are, whether they are for peace, against nuclear power, for liberation, or any other issue. We can know the hope of the poorest only through a long relationship with them. The Fourth World Movement built itself on this reality: to do everything possible to know what the poorest want, what they say, and why they say it. For me, there is nothing optional about this; it is an absolute necessity. To know what the very poor think is the essential experience, because it is also the experience of what Jesus Christ expects of us.

When you say, "Liberate which person in relation to which God?" you are thinking of God whom we can know through the Son who is incarnate in the poorest. To arrive at a Christian liberation theology, we would have to question the poorest.

What other path is there for a theology? We have to draw our reflection, as well as our practice, from the experience of the poorest people, not from an idea that we have of their existence but from the reality of their daily lives. Who are those who are living day and night in the heart of these miserable areas? And if they live there, are they in a state of constant listening as they would be in a university? And in what measure do such authentic witnesses inform our theology?

Our thoughts and our practice must be according to God's way. This forces us to draw our knowledge from the most rejected people; that is very difficult for us, for yet another reason we have not yet spoken about. In Europe, as I was telling you, these populations have never been questioned; the history of the underprivileged is a history of silence. It has been considered useless, and we have not tried to share the sensitivity of the very poor. The same goes more or less for the poorest of Latin America, even if there is much talk about them. They themselves do not bear witness, insofar as they have not been patiently questioned. Too rarely asked to bear witness, they are not able to develop a sense of public life, of the collective life, or of the community of all human beings. I do not see how Christians would have drawn a liberation theology from them.

Monsignor Proaño says, "The poor evangelize us," and you add, "No theology without them." There is no contradiction there.

I would add rather that there cannot be any theology without the most poor, and that the most poor do not teach us under just any conditions. Monsignor Proaño reminds us that in Latin America, most people are more or less in a state of slavery. Even there, to meet the Lord, we still need to go to the most oppressed. Shall we know where to find them, and under what conditions will they talk to us?

Let us take the example of Nicaragua. In Managua, during the struggles preceding the overthrow of the government, insurgent workers and revolutionary fighters were given shelter in the cathedral. Outside, people who were too poor to be revolutionary or even to be working were dying of hunger. The Church, then, was everywhere. Priests and religious sisters were not only feeding the fighters in the cathedral, they were also giving medical attention and sharing their supplies in the destitute areas of the city, where markets were no longer receiving goods. But these facts are hardly mentioned, and the Church itself is discreet about it. It is, however, important to know who are the people privileged by the Church and how it makes them guarantors of the Church's theology.

Later, also in Nicaragua, there was a different situation as regards the elimination of illiteracy. We were told that the people were liberated and that all were learning to read. This was not quite correct. In areas of extreme poverty, instructors had not yet arrived. They still have not arrived and, in any case, what does it mean to liberate the poor by bringing them the written word? By whom will the word be written?

Do you mean to say that Nicaragua is not a good example of the development of a theology of liberation?

Surely excellent examples exist in Nicaragua, but we are not fully informed about them. The Latin American bishops have reaffirmed that, wherever there was a choice to be made, we would find the Church always siding with the poor. The explosive state prevalent in this part of the world has given new impetus to theological research. But it is difficult to find out what means this research uses. It might be that, in Nicaragua, believers work out their theology through the fraternal act of teaching literacy. Does this encourage the poorest to speak up, to voice their thoughts, to reveal what lies at the heart of their lives? Such is my constant question.

In Western Europe, where school has been compulsory for many years, we see that even people who are learning to read and write can remain ignorant and not make progress if they are not called on to speak of their experience. In addition, they will believe that others want to hear what they have to say only if the people they speak with believe deeply in the importance, for themselves, of what the poor have to tell them. The value other people put on what you say makes you recognize that your thoughts are important. Then you will make a real effort to collect, sort out, and express your ideas.

Without this call to use the reading and writing skills they have learned, without being asked to say what makes them live and hope, people do not progress intellectually. They are not encouraged to learn more, to express themselves better, or to study further. It is of paramount importance for the poor to know that witnessing to their lives brings something vital to the whole of humanity. There, we are at the very heart of a liberation theology.

You say that, for the Church, the establishment of a liberation theology is a question of sharing life and thought with the most oppressed. Is that what John Paul II was thinking of when he said that all theologies were not necessarily of Christian inspiration?

The Pope said about freedom, "One must build one's personal and social life on freedom." Therefore, one must build the life of the Church on it as well. And he told us, during an encounter with some young people from the Fourth World in Rome, "The Church is the Church of Christ, who was born destitute." The Church is therefore inescapably, through Christ, linked to the condition of poverty. We explained this at the beginning of our conversations. We must now draw conclusions from this for theology.

Before speaking about liberation theology, we should speak about the theology of human beings as sons and daughters of God. The theology of men and women as God's offspring, God's children, is implicated here. Without a deep awareness of this, we will not listen to those who are the most deprived, the most difficult to meet, to understand, to accept, and to love as brothers or sisters. If we don't meditate on Christ poor, slandered, humiliated, and fallen, we will ask nothing of the very poor; we will speak in their place and we will organize liberation on a higher level, a level they will never be able to reach.

It is because we are not anchored in this truth—that we are all God's children—that the experience of others counts for so little with us. There is a sort of disdain, scorn, or even, perhaps, fear of others. This happens mainly with regard to the very poor who live outside our own lives, and who don't have the same understanding, the same means of expression, or even the same logic we do. We then consider their experiences and thoughts as worthless. I have often been amazed to see the contempt in which the liberators hold those to be liberated—not those of their own rank and class but others, the poorest in particular.

Liberation, yes, but whose liberation? The liberation of the children of God, certainly, but of God's most sullied and scarred children. With reference to which God? To the God of the Gospel, or else I really don't know what we are talking about.

You aren't thinking of a purely economic liberation, that is, a liberation from capitalism, good in itself?

The question is always who is being liberated. In Latin America, what is meant is economic and social liberation from a system in which Monsignor Proaño sees all people as more or less slaves. Among so many forms of oppression, which one should we combat? Among the many who are oppressed, who will spell out liberation for us?

If we talk of putting an end to oppression, then any manifestation of oppression must cease to exist. It cannot be a matter of relief only from some corporate injustice, or for some mineworkers, or for peasants working the land. Oppression, as such, must disappear. People must consequently pursue their encounter with the other person to the end, and make the other part of their lives, even the poorest. Otherwise nothing is achieved; oppression goes on, and we have only ourselves to blame. To love the other as ourselves, our love must embrace all that this entails, including deprivation comparable even to that of the most destitute person. If we do not accept all the consequences right to the end, we are just transposing exploitation. However, if we really persevere to the end with liberation, economic or otherwise, allying ourselves with the most disadvantaged, we are sooner or later allying ourselves with God.

Most of those who speak of liberation are young people. They do not doubt our sincerity in expressing basic principles, but, having excluded God, they do not understand why we don't go all the way. For us, however, God is not only the inspirer but also the reality of our principles. God is primary among the poorest. God is the poorest. As a society, we have excluded God from our social, economic, and political horizons. And we like to say that the gospel is not a political program. Thus, inevitably, we don't go so far as to include all people, notably the poorest. We are selective; we choose the poor who suit us, and God is absent: God is with those whom we reject.

For you, the poorest are not only a reference to God; they personify Jesus Christ as a poor man and also Jesus Christ free for us on earth. But God, free—what does that mean?

It is difficult to talk about God; this requires an experience as a community via the Church. Only the Church can talk about God. Each of us can only stammer when we try.

For me, the free God is a like a torrent that takes everything with it, all our lives, in an act of global love. Through relationship with God, the free person is the one who considers no one uninteresting. Such a person sweeps away all the obstacles that stand in the way of the gift of oneself and of understanding others. The freedom of God is such that even sin is no longer an obstacle. I have always thought that revolution can only mean that even sin does not stop God from loving us. Even hell cannot be totally frightening, since God cannot forget that we are God's children.

God cannot do other than take an interest in us. God is totally free to do so and to go to the very end. For us to follow God in this is a question of life or death. I can't see a liberation theology that is not based on the words of Saint John: "God is Love." God is not partially love; God is totally love. Similarly, the liberation of people has to be totally love; it needs to be freed of everything that prevents one from loving others—the poorest and the richest. The other day, I probably did not really answer your question about revolution. Now I can tell you that such a rupture between human beings cannot exist in the eyes of God. Jesus Christ died to avoid this.

One day, Jacques Chancel asked me in a radio interview, "Do you succeed in convincing people to follow you?" That is the question with which the Church is constantly trapped. Since you cannot claim that others follow you voluntarily, sooner or later you will have to use violence to come to terms with injustice. For my part, I can say in all sincerity that I have met many people who don't know about poverty. But I have never met anyone who, having discovered it, has remained indifferent.

Didn't the rich young man who questioned Jesus Christ go back home?

He didn't go all the way in his search. Above all, the Lord did not say it was necessary to start a revolution because nothing could be done with these people. He only remarked that it was more difficult for a rich person to get into heaven than for a camel to go through the eye of a needle. Christ never ceased to see the young man as someone who one day would be capable of it. For Jesus, the rich and the poor would join him, not in the Kingdom of Heaven, but on this earth, to start the Kingdom in this earthly life. You might say I am indulging in pietism and that I am referring to the poor and to the rich in relation to the afterlife. That is not my intention at all. It is simply that I don't believe we have the right to despair of others. Even in this life, people want to get together; they aspire to peace, to understanding, and to mercy. To negate another human being goes against human nature.

I have spent my life wanting to convince people, and I have often been discouraged because I expected from everyone else what the poor expect from me. I did not realize that each person brings what he or she can to a struggle, whatever the struggle. I expected they would all act like the Fourth World volunteers, accepting the poorest as the only ones capable of teaching them about God. I imposed a mission on them that was not necessarily theirs. In expecting too much of them, I did not try to discover the efforts they were already making.

Since then, I have always asked myself whether those who consider revolution inevitable—in Latin America and elsewhere—are certain of having used other available means to convince the wealthy. If we had the patience and the perseverance with the rich that we claim to have with the poor, and if we made the same effort to understand them, I think situations in the world would change. We ourselves would be more loving and more committed, and the world would change. You will ask me if I want the poor to continue to suffer in the meantime. It is always the same pitfall: the misfortune of the poor cannot wait. This is true, so we must share ourselves with them without further delay. If we took the burden of their suffering upon ourselves and had no other concern, we ourselves would be the first to share the price of our patience with the affluent. Who would dare say that to join the inhabitants of the poorest areas would not change the world for them entirely? If we think that giving our lives to the poorest would not change theirs, then we do not understand them, and we do them harm. In any case, what does it mean to free the poor, if not to offer them our personal freedom? The important thing is to devote it entirely to bringing them back to the feast. They should join not only the Church but also the unions, daily activities, and the struggle of those who fight for a new society.

One might say that being God's children is like a current inside the torrent of the love of God. And this love does not carry certain people only, leaving the others behind. The distinctive feature of the water source is to lose itself in the mass of water. The trickle of water that flows from the source of the torrent is visible only to those who take the time to look and who wait to see the drops gushing forth.

In truth, human beings are very vain. They want to carry out the work of God and they say, "This will be done in our generation or never." This is an error. In reality, each generation carries on a part of the liberation. We must know how to recognize it, to receive it, and put it to good use. The tragedy is that we do not know how to assess things. We are forever saying that attempts fail because they do not turn out as we would want them to. If we had the humility and respect to look much closer, we would see some progress.

I have known people who joined the Movement and then left. Ten years later, they would tell me, "You know, I didn't stay, but I never looked at the world in the same way again." Just as society imposes its own salvation on the poorest with messages such as, "You will do things in such a way and not in any other," so we want to change society by imposing on it the changes we have chosen. This is not launching liberation; it is replacing one type of oppression with another.

Wouldn't our realization that we are all children of God enable us to have great patience? Do you think that Christians who are indignant at the poverty of their brothers and sisters can accept that kind of patience?

I think so, as long as this patience does not resemble either a wait-and-see policy or action moving at a snail's pace. God is always the one who "breaks loose from all moorings" or who "knocks over every sea wall." God is the torrent that surges constantly through the centuries. I can assure you that our lives can be a part of this and can contribute to the liberation of the poor, starting now, as long as we don't keep our progress to ourselves. The poorest have the right to know that all people, whoever they may be, are faced with the same choice as that of the young rich man. It is an internal and also an external choice if we are ready to pay attention to it. Jesus Christ teaches hope and confirms that hope is possible and effective. So what right have we to teach the poor revolution, which is the very expression of despair? How can we do such great harm to them? Everyone, rich or poor, is in search of God. In the course of this search, wouldn't each person look for harmony with all other human beings? The poor are the first to aspire to peace, which is the salvation of human beings. But revolutions are suicidal for all.

When we look closely at people and systems, trying to see their best attributes, we discover the extraordinary fact that, deep down, they all want the same thing. It is as if, regardless of the paths chosen, everyone is committed to the same fate: the search for human fulfillment. We have no right to deny anyone his desire for human fulfillment. This does not prevent us from seeing deviations and denouncing perversity. But our main effort should lie elsewhere. If we believe that God is alive, that God is all-powerful, constantly re-emerging, our main challenge will be to witness God's strength wherever it emerges in any person. Continuous protest cannot be a protest against human beings; it is only a reminder of the inadequacy of their actions. It is unthinkable that such protest could be hostile to humans or despairing of them.

Your Movement exists on all the continents and you travel to all cultures; you call on people under every type of government. In your opinion, does the best in all people lead them necessarily to the God of the gospel? If not, the free God whom you talk about would be a parochial God, whereas for us he is absolute. Can God be absolute in the eyes of Buddhism?

By asking the question in this way, you suppose that the Good News was adapted to the culture of a certain era, in a certain area of the world. The notion of a "Judeo-Christian" civilization seems to confirm this. But I think this is a mistake.

You ask yourself whether Jesus Christ crucified is conceivable in a Buddhist culture and religion. I would reply that this was not conceivable within the Jewish culture. The son of a king making himself poor for a time was something thinkable. But the son of a king dying like a pauper contradicted both history and legend. Traditionally, love did not reach such extremes, and history took a happy turn at the right time. Thus, the gathering of all people around Jesus Christ is a mystery for all cultures. It is a matter for God, the mystery of God's love: we cannot know what forms this will take tomorrow. Up to now, this love has always led us, in one way or another, to the poorest. God has shown his love through Jesus Christ in a way that is not only original but also absolute, since Christ stood out because of his own destitution.

For my part, I am sure of two things. At a given time in history, Jesus Christ, son of God, came to bring humanity the essential responses it needed and clamored for. Jesus Christ is the apex of God's revelations and responses. These responses are still offered to us today, and I am called to apply them by living them myself. This twofold certainty is sufficient for me. Rather than try to know how God speaks in other religions, I must love others to such an extent that they share with me the best of themselves.

To tell the truth, I have never asked myself the question of how my Islamic brothers and my Buddhist friends were going to encounter one another around God. I am all the more confident that there are already signs of unity. We are discovering it in East Senegal; around villages under the shadow of starvation; around handicapped children in a population immersed in extreme poverty, in the Upper Volta.[18] We find this unity around families in Thailand who are among the most disparaged because of their destitution. In concrete terms, I have never met, among the more privileged, any person who didn't show interest in or who had nothing to say to their poorest sisters and brothers. On the contrary, we exchanged the best in each of us with these people.

I am speaking here of concrete experience: at the grass-roots level, right in the action, we have never come across any religion or ideology that defends the rich. On the other hand, we meet people everywhere who admit that the poorest are absent from their lives and that it should not be so. No religion considers this absence as willed by God. There again, we should keep in mind that Jesus Christ has already established the unity to which he invites us. Unity has been achieved: it is up to us to take the path that leads to it: the most worn-out person will show us the way. That person is the path and the unity.

The drive to liberate the poor through interpersonal encounters, rather than by revolution, has led you to found a volunteer corps that includes all denominations. Though it serves as a sample of the community at large, is it a convincing model for the national societies of our time?

It is more a model for a way of life or a way of sharing in the deepest sense: you are a Jew, I will be a Jew with you; you are a Muslim, we shall be Muslims together; you do not believe in God but you believe in humanity, I shall go with you to the logical conclusion of faith in humans. This goes far beyond mutual respect. During a volunteer meeting, a volunteer who does not believe in God was the first to proclaim that the poor have a right to a spiritual life.

By this he meant that spirituality did not belong only to believers. Moreover he said, "Those of you who believe in God, why are you waiting to give the Fourth World the best of yourselves? I, a non-believer, am asking you to take your convictions to their logical conclusion."

This volunteer showed himself to be the firmest believer in humans. Seeing the volunteer corps as capable of retaining and uniting people from such multiple and diverse horizons led Cardinal Marty to say, "Perhaps this Movement, which is not of the Church, is nevertheless an authentic expression of the Church of tomorrow."

And this brings me back to liberation theology. It is not an amendment to theology but a deepening of it. And this is a blessing for the poorest. They cannot understand that those who possess the means of unity and peace do not make good use of them. When they speak of a better future, when their children talk of hope among themselves, the same words always crop up: "People should understand. Everyone should be hand in hand." What right have we not to take this desire seriously? Who allows us to propose struggles and revolutions that the poor themselves have not developed or chosen? When will we stop thinking on their behalf, closing the door to any original contribution from them?

Those who propose struggle to the poor have perhaps not chosen them either. Their realism prevents them from believing in a political conversion of the rich, especially in Latin America.

I am not in a position to make a judgment about this. The volunteers are present in Indian villages so abandoned that they appear to be beyond any proposed effort. For us, the point is how to reach them in out-of-the-way places in the mountains, to bring them to the feast. How do we let ourselves be converted by them? And what are their own hopes? Are we capable of returning together to society to rebuild it?

In any case, the more we want to try to change society, the more we forget the anguish of the poor, who also want to be transformed. "Bring the Good News to the poor" is a requirement for more than one reason. Jesus Christ knew they could not even imagine freedom as long as they were—and still are—imprisoned in their deprivation. We have already mentioned their immeasurable need for pardon. They need to believe in themselves if they are to be free before God and other people. Perhaps one has to live among them to really understand this suffering, greater than any other: the pain of feeling inferior to everyone and even to oneself, being always undeserving of love and justice, believing in peace and yet being incapable of achieving peace. It is quite legitimate to want to free society from violence, greed, and dishonesty. But haven't the poor the need and the right to be the first ones freed from all this?

We see a society in which success for one person means defeat for another. We chase other persons out so we can take their place, or we belittle them so that they don't take ours. We live in the midst of so much antagonism. Under these conditions, it is difficult for us to realize that society and humanity live by a spirituality that sheds light on our antagonism. Educated people are always forging a spiritual life for themselves, whatever their beliefs. They consequently find reasons for living—for example, humanity or justice—that are beyond themselves and that make them grow. If necessary, they find justification for their selfish behavior, such as: I am acting in the name of freedom of enterprise; I am collecting the just reward for being an industrious and thrifty person. They also find compensations, such as: God loves me, God will help me. But the poorest have no means of building up a life or an inner security in this way. The worst oppression is, indeed, that we have not shared our education, our spirituality, or our God with the poor. And we are all responsible for this oppression.

The poor are as prone as anyone else to humiliate their neighbors, to defame them, and to envy someone who has received help. As a result of the pain of having their own children taken away, they are capable of informing social services about another family who does not feed the children adequately. This goes together with the acts of kindness and generosity we already mentioned. But no one comes to tell them that looking beyond themselves will lead them toward God, and that, as children of God, they are journeying to their Father. The disciples were cowards, and their behavior was the perfectly realistic behavior of poor people confronted by persons in control. The Lord made them understand that they could be agents of salvation. We, ourselves, abandon the poorest to the same weaknesses as other people by depriving them of the spirituality that would enable them to cope with these weaknesses. Therefore, I cannot understand this proposed liberation for the poor which does not allow them to enter a new society, sure of themselves, free, and holding their heads high. One cannot start a revolution with slaves, Lenin said. In my opinion, one does not build a new society with people who are laden with guilt and shame.

Have we gone too far in portraying the poor as "the just"?

I speak mainly about the very poor. They are not portrayed as the "just"; on the contrary, they are called the "bad poor." When they quarrel and betray one another, we turn this into a weapon against them: "Can't you see that these people are incapable of living together and of behaving like honest people? They even steal from each other!" Their difficulties legitimize our rejection of them: "You see, you can't do anything with those people." In France and elsewhere, social scientists have contributed to this way of condemning the Fourth World. One of them did this in the Noisy-le-Grand camp, asserting that the families did not accept living together, that they attacked one another and stole from one another.

For you, the "liberation" of the poor, therefore, means liberation from sin. That is a position some would call reactionary.

I would call reactionaries those who promote a narrow concept of human rights, reducing them to civil and political liberties, which, if taken alone, are completely ineffectual for the poor. The freedom of political participation by itself leads to a scandalous enslavement of populations if those who possess the means to think and speak deprive them of education, spirituality, inner security, and self-assurance. This amounts to despising the poor, putting them back in the lowest ranks and making them the recipients of our benevolence. It is the opposite of liberation.

For me liberation means, above all, evangelizing the poorest by placing them at the center of the evangelization of the world. Jesus Christ not only says, "Go off the beaten track"; he requires that we bring the blind and the lame to the feast. To evangelize the most impoverished does not mean that we trap ourselves with them, right where they are. It means restoring them to their rightful place at the heart of the gospel, where Jesus Christ placed Lazarus, the Samaritan woman, and the shepherds of Bethlehem.

If we are to break with the past, we must do it in the same way Jesus Christ did, through a cultural revolution. I strongly believe in cultural revolution. I told you that Jesus Christ introduced cultural revolution into the world through his incarnation, life, and death. Nothing in the culture of his time had prepared the minds of the people for this; even the prophets did not succeed. The way Jesus revealed himself to humankind was incomprehensible to everyone from the start. He completely upset all the ideas, plans, and stereotypes of his time. He made a clean break with all that, causing a cultural rift with the Jewish people. Christianity broke off from Judaism; it did not preserve it in the hearts and minds of believers.

But Jesus Christ did not merely herald a cultural revolution; he called for a culture that would be a permanent revolution. Even today, no civilization has been able to fully assume the Christian revolution, that is, to really give priority to the poorest.

The cultural revolution can also be violent.

The cultural revolution of Christianity does violence to generally accepted ideas but not to human beings. I don't believe it needs to do violence to them. Christ has made his life and his death the culmination—and, at the same time, the sign—of a revolution in minds and hearts. This revolution has been completed, and Jesus has left us his Church so that everyone will have the opportunity, in their turn, to join him. There is no one to whom the Church can say: Revolution has happened without you; we have done this for you or against you, without your involvement.

However, in order to commit ourselves with the Church to this ongoing revolution, which is open to everyone, we are forced to reinvent the form it will take, as well as the education of human persons. We have to rethink its content and means, and designate the teachers, because to evangelize for liberation and to bring others to follow Christ, means to prepare hearts and minds and to ensure the best conditions for this. The Church has done this throughout its history and has constantly adapted its behavior, its liturgy, its language, and its institutions to those of the society of its time. It has always done so with a profound respect for the development of humanity, guiding it but not preceding it. It changes its language as people change their understanding, with respect for their gradual progress. Moreover, because of this, the Church is accused of lagging behind and of trying to catch up with the world. This is false. Isn't the Church the source of all the major changes of vision we take part in? Perhaps it is not the only source, but it is certainly not the least abundant. The Church is sometimes behind in language or behavior. This is normal because it is not of this world. But no one can deny that it is always in the forefront on behalf of the poor because Jesus Christ places himself in the forefront of all the poor, and the Church has to join him as a poor person. The Church does not have to bring itself up to date with regard to the world, but it has to adapt itself with regard to the poor whom the world doesn't accept as yet. In this way, too, by always leading people further ahead, it continuously liberates. Christians, like anyone else throughout history, tend to come to a halt in history by making a certain poor person the goal in their search for poverty. By doing so they settle down in a particular position and become trapped in struggles the justice of which cannot be denied, but which are often already outdated. The Church says that there is no time for this now, that in order to go forward we have to shake off our chains and everything that weighs us down.

Can you explain this to me in concrete terms?

Concretely, the Church must make use of all the experiences relating to extreme poverty that it has accumulated throughout history, so as to gain a better understanding of poverty in its present-day forms. The Church and its constituents have acquired a knowledge which has to bear fruit. Our society itself, over the centuries, has retained the memory of discoveries about the poorest, that is, the excluded. I have told you about the lineage of the poor, and I told you that their history had not been told. Yet we possess a buried memory and very real experiences. The gospel is there to help us put them in order and to shed new light on them. Realities that were still misunderstood and even incomprehensible yesterday are no longer so today. Think of the way in which we speak now, not simply of poor, developing countries, but of the poorest countries among these. It is normal today to recognize that the poorest countries are not those which are exploited but those with which we don't even establish a relationship as property owners with capital to exploit. Suddenly memory is aroused, and we become the conveyers of a mass of ideas and of the experience of what it means to be excluded.

You seem to say that humanity is progressing.

It is progressing; that is obvious. Its sensitivity progresses; people educate each other and constantly acquire new insights, new values, and new behaviors. We have fallen into the habit of greatly devaluing human beings, and there is a certain consistency in our view. We have become cynical about humanity because of its economic cruelty, its armaments, and its squandering of natural resources. We forget to mention what great progress it is to be able to talk of nature, to demonstrate against arms, or to militate for a new international economic order. Never before have our ideals been placed so high.

We still see revolution as the only means of promoting world progress. When we look at it through the eyes of the poorest, we realize that revolution only does away with elements that were already falling apart. Whatever makes progress now, has made progress before. And people made progress by relying on experiences that were patiently accumulated and written into the common memory. The reason why the Movement was so eager to write the history of the poor was to incorporate it into our collective memory, confident that humanity would make it bear fruit.

I do not believe in the sort of degradation that would make people worse than before. They acquire, they experiment, they fail, and their failures enable them to advance as much as their successes do. I don't merely believe in progress; I can see it.

Despite the Gulag, despite the extermination of the Jews? Haven't there been backward steps which, to say the least, are infinitely regrettable?

Atrocities always remain terrible; animal nature is always part of our makeup. We will always remain capable of the worst, and we have to expect this. I claim that human sensitivity is progressing, not that every person is on a par with that level of sensitivity. The people of God progresses, but the obligation to attain the ideal remains with the individual. People are capable of perceiving this ideal at certain moments in history. This is not blind optimism on my part. I don't see how we could be misled about the permanent progress of our ideals.

The poorest are not misled in this regard. They remind us of all the benefits acquired in our common humanity, in democracy, and in human rights, which have gradually spread but have not reached the poorest. In your opinion, would the message of Dom Helder Camara have had the same impact fifty years ago that it does today? Would he have been invited to speak to the general public in Europe? This kind of progress removes any justifications for oppression.

We must measure the progress of humanity by the questions it asks itself. We see the changing vision of human persons in the answers people give each other. The Gulags have always existed, but today people are more aware of the atrocities. We each feel less human because of the cruelties of a Pinochet, because of oppression in Afghanistan, or a massacre in Cambodia. We can no longer say, "That does not concern me. What has that got to do with me?" Today, freedom demands that we proclaim these violations to be the fault of all humanity.

Has Cain become ashamed?

Cain can no longer hide. Society no longer accepts fratricide, and this adds something to the memory and thought of human beings. Tomorrow other misdeeds will become unbearable in their turn.

We are at present witnessing a sort of break in arrogance. Yesterday in the West, we still believed that poverty had vanished. We were proud of our systems of solidarity and social welfare, and we thought we had succeeded doing what no other society had ever succeeded doing before. Our vision is still not clear; it is clouded with stereotypes, prejudices, and preconceived ideas. We are only at a first stage of our re-education in humility. We still remain very arrogant with regard to peoples in developing countries, convinced that our democratic experience and our scientific knowledge make us the intellectual guides for the world. We willingly say—through a sort of false humility, without really believing in it—that the poor have a great deal to teach us. But there is some explanation for this false pretense at humility. We feel we can no longer set ourselves up as masters of the world. This is no longer accepted by our peers.

Also inscribed in our memory is the fact that we have searched in vain for salvation through structures, while economizing on personal effort. The fact that institutions become non-egalitarian and exclusive, contrary to the legislator's initial intention, is a discovery of our time that prepares us to reread our history in the lives of those excluded from our institutions.

Our rediscovered humility can teach us a new way of looking at the poor. For generations, we have pointed a finger at them and asserted that they were uninterested, inefficient, and responsible for their own condition. We need time to transform ourselves, to change our way of looking at people, and to purify ourselves. We should have as much indulgence for humanity as we have for our children, in view of the fact that humanity does not develop or change all at once.

12.

The Consecrated Life

Gilles Anouil: In conclusion, what direction would you like to see the Church take?

Father Joseph Wresinski: I have stated all along the wish that haunts me: that the Church identify with the dreadful and repulsive poverty of our time; that it identify anew with itself, winning the love of the poorest and transmitting this love to the world. May its message to the world be filled with the love the poor will have for it because they will recognize in the Church the face of Christ, downcast, swollen, and soiled by spittle. That is the Christ who is risen. In the real life of the most rejected persons, God not only expresses but reveals God, makes God known—not as an object or an idea but as a being to be loved. I wish with all my heart that the Church might experience this and proclaim it today.

I am sure the Church will know how to adapt evangelization, basing it on men and women committed to the world of extreme poverty. The Church will know how to find new forms that will embrace not only poverty but also destitution. The world has initiated many institutions to respond to human problems. These institutions are undoubtedly well-meaning, but they have also become barriers against the intrusion of the poor, and their programs remain ineffective as regards the poor. But the Church can and must let itself be invaded. It can let itself be forced to reinvent ways to love the poorest; ways to love them so that they know through other flesh-and-blood human beings that love is possible and that it brings freedom.

The Church must send into this "no man's land" of destitution thirsty for human beings, some "go-betweens" who will bring back to it the families of the Fourth World. It is only under this condition that the Church can say, "You are all children of God, brothers and sisters with a common destiny, which prevents you from considering anyone an inferior to be rejected." The Church can only speak from experience; solidarity has to be experienced within it, and because of this it must send men and women to the Fourth World.

You are saying that in the Church, the institution must embrace love. How can rules and love become one?

This is what the Church has been attempting to do for two thousand years. But, in order that the rules not destroy or paralyze, a considerable human investment is needed. Without this, even the Church, like any other institution, would be primarily characterized by prohibitions for the poor. However, it is indebted to them for the education of love, an education that prepares us to live according to the commandments of God. The Church is totally vulnerable in a world where it can impose nothing and where its message is often ridiculed. Only the poor are as dependent as the Church is. Together, they can rediscover again and again that only love counts.

Today the Church does not proclaim the primacy of love as it did through its daily life when it was continually present in the lives of people. It was then better situated to talk about the love of God because it was present not only in people's struggles but also in their lives. Priests did not feel it was pointless to take time to visit the families; nuns did not feel unneeded in the schools. They all represented a Church that was confident, mediatory, a friend, and an educator. Obviously, we don't have to go back to the old ways, but, in order to achieve its mission, the Church must send into the world men and women who are totally dedicated to those personal relationships and devoted to uniting the best of themselves with the infinite tenderness of God.

You say devoted. Are you thinking of the vocation of a priest or nun? Isn't that again going against the grain of public opinion, which considers that all believers are equally called to mission?

This is what the Church has to provide, not in compliance with the opinion of affluent men and women but in accordance with the needs of the destitute because these are also its own needs. I often think of one thing the Church requires of a priest: celibacy. It places us in a very uncomfortable and perilous situation in the modern world. Why? Some claim it is only prescribing a rule. That is not true. The Church has a very longstanding relationship with people and with the poor in particular. Consequently, it knows that if we are to witness the deprivation of the Lord, it will not be through the deprivation of material goods alone. Material deprivation is not insignificant, but it is very little compared to that of our own flesh. That is where we receive the stigmata of Christ crucified. Celibacy is nothing other than a testimony to the profound respect that the Church has for humanity. It shows that it is ready to lose something of its essential humanness, so as to gain "something more" of a different order.

The Church, therefore, has good reasons for calling and consecrating those who dedicate themselves in this way to the Lord. It must also point out to them clearly those who, on earth, are Christ imprisoned, starving, naked, and sick, and on whom they can bestow their love. And the Church must be very careful that these persons receive a truly exemplary training. This should be a training of the heart for love and for a permanent commitment because that is what the poorest hunger for, reduced as they are to a state of absolute inferiority.

You asked me whether a vocation or a special mission was necessary to the poorest and to the Church. I would reply that those who have consecrated their lives to God are, in the Church's eyes, the first ones called to love God through the most destitute men and women. But this won't happen through the newly organized kind of charity which has replaced almsgiving. The Church must reinvent the form of personal response, which in a way was part of the traditional charity of times past. It must again find the form of constant commitment that was part of almsgiving, or rather of which almsgiving was a part. Almsgiving still exists, but it is now organized by large, more anonymous mutual aid institutions. In the Church, we haven't maintained the physical presence that was a response to the anguish of the Fourth World and its need for peace.

You should know, furthermore, that the poorest make no mistake about our commitments. They feel it deeply when laypeople protect themselves, demanding personal life, fulfillment, and guarantees for their future. Then the poor cannot fully trust them or expect real change from them. Very poor families have often voiced this to me, and yet they accept these limitations. They understand the difficulty laypeople have in committing their lives more fully. However, I have never seen them accepting any reservations on the part of the clergy. The families cannot allow that priests or religious people limit their time or use their communities as a protection from them.

In my experience, the families of the Fourth World know the difference; it is as if they realize that nuns and priests must be the hidden, obscure, and humble part of the Church. They do not understand the restrictions often imposed on nuns, requiring them, for example, to spend every weekend in their communities. They resent the fact that their neighborhood is not considered a viable place for the existence of those they call "the Good Sisters" and that others can set limits on their spiritual and human commitment.

In my opinion, the Fourth World teaches us that the presence of priests and nuns in the territory of the poor is valid only if they dedicate themselves to the families in complete trust and without reservation, as is the case for missionaries or for those who dedicate themselves to the world of work.

You aren't thinking of a new mendicant order?[19]

I didn't say that priests had to become beggars. Mendicant orders were a protest against the world but not a direct reply to poverty at all. In passing, I will express my regret at no longer seeing religious people from mendicant orders going from door to door. It would remind us that poverty at the heart of humanity eludes any social organization or structure. This practice remains prevalent in vast areas of the world, and it does no harm to justice; on the contrary, it is beneficial. We had to abandon those ancient forms of protest against the social, economic, and political order. We have not been able, however, to replace them with other ways of witnessing to Christ's life and of acknowledging the inadequacy of our structures. The poorest are alone and more ashamed than before at having to solicit their share of alms.

But this is not what I wanted to say. I was thinking of priests, monks, and nuns, envoys of a Church whose raison d'être is forgiveness and which gives them the mission of living it with the poorest. Indeed, forgiveness is the true liberation, the freedom that is essential and absolutely necessary to human beings. This is not an idea but the very message conveyed by the families of the Fourth World every day of their lives. I told you they live the message of the gospel in the most concrete way. It is time to tell them this and to help them live it with joy.

This is not just a matter for the Church alone or for its ministers. I am deeply convinced that it concerns every human being and that all people, whatever their belief, can devote their life to this. And I believe that the gift of a life carries the same value regardless of who gives it—the same price is paid, the same liberation occurs. But to persevere in this deprivation of self requires considerable and continuous training and support. Others outside the Church can choose to give of themselves and to create the necessary training and support. The Church has no choice; it is dedicated to the poorest; it is poverty. The community of the Church, and the training that it gives, exist first of all for the poor. We shall never insist enough on the idea of the mission it has received. If the Church did not go to the Fourth World, it would behave like the foolish virgins because it would not make its immeasurable inheritance bear fruit. I am not saying that the Church will reach the Fourth World effortlessly. It has received a mission that is beyond the human strength.

The mission is first of all a call to human persons, then a mission of training and support. Think how difficult it is to leave the world, to leave the fold to look for the lost sheep. Think of all the ways in which intelligence, heart, and soul tempt us by making us think we can do everything for the world by staying in the world. We all receive today the mission of liberation, justice, and peace. The world gives us a guilty conscience if we do not put all our energy into these without ceasing. What can the voice and the strength of a calling from the poorest be, in the midst of the world's noisy demands? And what can be the appeal of devoting one's life at a time when the gift of self is often seen as going against one's right to fulfillment? To devote one's life is a human right, and to be able to devote it freely is the absolute right of the poorest. But in our time it is not easy to proclaim that.

The Church finds it difficult enough—and will find it increasingly so—to obtain the necessary training and support for those who respond to such a call. At a time when so many call themselves experts in human affairs, at a time when everyone is supposed to be a liberator and a strategist in liberation, how can one highlight the unique education offered by the Church? The world today allows any number of daring innovations, any number of experiences, and each person feels invested with a mission. Humanity seems to be fully responsible; what we witness nowadays is an unprecedented step forward. But there is the other side of the coin: we find it hard to accept any training unless at a technological level. Since human beings are experts in humanity and responsible for their brothers and sisters, they know what they have to do. What would training and consecration provide that is not already there? We do not want to remember that the Church has a legacy of love for the poorest, and that this love has to be learned because it goes against nature and requires practice and much support.

Although we no longer wish to remember this legacy, we continue to feel it. Isn't that what makes the laity—people like myself—unsatisfied? Many of us are fascinated by the unity of life, a sort of absolute unity that religious life offers. We are dissatisfied at not having made that commitment. But it is very easy for us to cast aside this thought; life offers us such an abundance of less demanding interests.

These are valid interests, which can also provide you with moments of grace. All this is very positive; but it should not dissuade us from teaching people how to follow an ideal all the way. And this should begin very early in life, from preschool and the first school years on.

Isn't this precisely the justification for Christian schools? This justification is far more concrete and solid than one might think. It is not only a question of a family's freedom of choice. It is a question of the Church's freedom of being, of the right of children and of the poorest persons to knowledge. The Church, which has educated the poorest faithfully throughout the centuries, has to continue to teach. Throughout the ages it has continuously opposed and fought against the ignorance of the poor. For the Church, it is a question of life and death. It must again bring education to places where schooling is lacking. It's not a question of replacing state education but of bringing it even to the street, to the slums, and all disadvantaged areas. The Church must set the example in this—all the more so because it is the only institution in our countries to have and to be the memory of the poor. No other institution can pretend to be this.

But the most important motivation is to share with young children what they alone can understand: absolute, uncompromising, and total sincerity. Children and the Church's destiny are linked; there has been an understanding between them throughout time. Children have the right to live with a passion of which we adults are no longer always capable; that is, to live with the absolute and constantly to be on familiar terms with it. Here's where the willingness and the commitment to renounce the world on behalf of the poorest and the rejected begins.

Do you speak of religious commitment? You say it is up to the Church to provide ways, but aren't you yourself thinking of a religious life consecrated by the Church?

I don't know what forms such a commitment can take or what seal the Church will use. All I know is that the Fourth World has a pressing need for totally committed men and women. Also, these men and women need to know that their mission comes from a community; that they are sent and given support by a community that will guarantee their training and faithfulness. Poverty—we can never say it enough—poverty is not a unifying factor; of itself it will never be a common denominator. It does not of itself lead to a way of thinking or to an ethic. It leads to activity that can soon become activism, with the risk of destroying the persons involved. This is because, by itself, an action does not unify; it divides people. Those sent by the Church to the field need a strong community.

Doesn't the greatest strength of the Church lie in constant meditation and adoration. What is the place of contemplatives in relation to poverty?

They serve a unique purpose. From the very beginning, in Noisy-le-Grand, I had hoped that men and women would come with the sole preoccupation to pray, adore, contemplate, and bring silence and peace—a peace one could feel. You can't imagine how much Fourth World families need this. It is essential to introduce into their disturbed world this element of stability, of lasting peace.

Is a mutual exchange possible between two worlds that are poles apart?

They are not poles apart; one is full of what the other lacks most. One just needs to be there. I have often asked myself what was the use of the Church praying, adoring, and singing the glory of God, carrying the prayer of the poor, if the poor don't know about this and cannot be united with it. The poor will be able to be very united when they can make this prayer of the Church their own, when one day they recognize themselves in it and are carried by it. When I told you how much I wanted the Church to identify with the extreme poverty of our time, I was also thinking of this contemplative presence, which is indispensable.

This presence is quite possible; it does great harm to the poor to think otherwise. A mutual welcome is assured, provided that the Church makes itself known. I cannot tell you how many women who were brought up by nuns and who have since led very eventful lives, have said to me, "Father, I can't tell you how much I regret not becoming a nun." This was not a vague desire, nor was it a remark whose significance they didn't grasp. In their childhood, they were close to nuns who prayed; they felt the silence of peace and the fullness of contemplation.

We have relegated contemplatives to a world outside ours for historic reasons. Yet they are the only ones who are able to proclaim: I am in the world yet I am not of the world. Only contemplatives can remain unaltered, uncompromised, unshaken by a passing fad or worldly idea. In the past, contemplative orders lived in rural areas, not to escape from the world but rather because people—and especially the poor—lived there. Today contemplatives are no longer present where the life of the poor unfolds.

Perhaps the contemplatives are the least loved and the most misunderstood persons in the modern Church. More than ever, they are those who live Gethsemane to its fullness. Everything happened so fast on the Mount of Olives, but the whole of redemption was accomplished. The seemingly useless prayer of human persons, the prayer that is not listened to or understood or accepted, the prayer by which human persons are saved: that's what contemplatives are in the Church. In this way, they are the prayer of the poorest who, themselves, are the Church.

Endnotes

Preface

1. The name in French is ATD Quart Monde (which will be translated throughout as "Fourth World Movement"). Why this double title? In Chapter 7, Father Joseph explains that the first association was created by a few people from the camp who chose to call themselves "Group for European Action and Culture." They were refused incorporation because of this title and the fact that some of their members had been in trouble with the law. Says Father Joseph, "I had to find a few people who had never been to jail." He turned to a friend and together they founded a "new" association. The friend asked that it be called "Aide à Toute Détresse" (Help for All in Distress). The families agreed, since the objectives would not change. Later the people themselves adopted the name "Fourth World." They had learned that Dufourny de Villiers, at the time of the French Revolution, had coined the term "Quart Monde" to designate the vast numbers of persons who did not belong to any of the recognized "estates" of French society.

2. Allies are women and men from all walks of life who decide to stand with the poorest as members of the Fourth World Movement. They learn from the Movement what life in poverty is really like, then spread that knowledge in all spheres of society and put their know-how and connections at the disposal of the Movement, in the struggle against extreme poverty and social exclusion. The Alliance, an association of allies, brings them together and is a platform for action in the wider society.

Volunteers constitute the Fourth World Volunteer Corps. They are committed long-term and full-time to the work of the Movement. After one year's training they begin working and living in small teams, sharing the daily lives of the very poor, joining in their struggle, and trying to establish partnership with others. At the present time there are 350 volunteers, who come from five continents and from many different professional, social, religious, and cultural backgrounds. There are teams of volunteers in 22 countries. All volunteers receive the same subsistence stipend, and they try to live as simply as possible. They change location and mission every three to six

185

years, taking their turn in the tasks of organization, research, and fund raising. The structures of both the volunteer corps and the Movement itself change to meet the needs of the time. In 1999, one volunteer, Eugen Brand (Switzerland), was appointed Secretary-General in charge of the whole Movement, to be assisted by two other volunteers, Susan Devins (U.S.A.) and Bruno Couder (France). An advisory committee is made up of a group of the longest serving volunteers.

Introduction

3. What follows is a publisher's account of why this introduction is composed of a brief history of the text and a poignant memoir of his life by Father Joseph himself. The "we" in the first paragraph of this section refers to members of the publishing house. The text was prepared for publication by Charles Ehlinger, a staff member of Le Centurion, because Gilles Anouil was in Japan at the time.

4. The "we" in this subtitle refers to Father Joseph and his early friends, several of whom became permanent volunteers. See Chapters 7 and 9.

Chapter 1: The Church Is the Church of the Poor

5. For the remainder of the book, the questions and comments by Gilles Anouil are italicized; the reflections and responses of Father Joseph Wresinski are not.

6. The phrase "Cour des Miracles" is drawn from Victor Hugo's *Hunchback of Notre Dame*. The term refers to subterranean areas in Paris, near the great Cathedral, which were gathering spaces and refuge for marginal persons—criminals, derelicts, the unfortunate and the poorest. Literally, it means "Court of Miracles." The term implies both irony and indestructible hope.

Chapter 2: The Life of the Poorest Is a Source of Grace

7. Madame Soleil is the name of a well-known fortune teller in France.

Chapter 3: To Be Incarnated in a People

8. "Mission de France" refers to an evangelization movement of the forties directed toward the vast numbers of unchurched but often baptized Catholics in France. Many, of course, were also destitute. Father Joseph refers to them in the introductory section headed, "We had only ourselves to offer." Many of the protagonists of the "Mission" became the inspiration for American activists, especially in the Chicago area of the United States. Cf. *Is France*

Pagan? by Claire Huchet Bishop.

9. This literally means "Catholic Emergency Aid." This was a French organization concerned with helping both foreign and domestic poor. Comparable organizations in the United States are Catholic Relief Services for aid to countries outside the U.S.; Association of Catholic Charities for domestic poverty; and Conferences of the Society of St. Vincent de Paul, which are active in individual church parishes.

Chapter 5: Where Do They Come From?
10. Father Joseph mentions by name this one founder of an orphanage in the nineteenth century. The *Catholic Encyclopedia* in its first edition (1913; Robert Appleton Company/The Encyclopedia Press, New York) surveys only some of the institutes that sprang up between 1799 and 1809, remarking: "Such was the fruit of a few years of religious revival... the list could easily be continued through the years that followed" (Vol. 9, pp. 322-325).

Chapter 6: Sub-Proletarian Workers, Suffering Face of the Working World
11. These are names of low-cost housing sites. Omitted from the English text are "Tergnier and Fargnier"— in northern France.

Chapter 8: The First Allies, or the Courage to Commit Oneself
12. "Help for All in Distress."
13. Périer-Daville was a journalist with *Le Figaro*, a national French daily.

Chapter 9: "Put Out Into the Deep and Let Down Your Nets for a Catch"
14. Upper Volta is now Burkina Faso and it is so designated in subsequent publications of the Fourth World. See the list at the end of this book.

Chapter 10: "Priority Given to the Poorest": What Does It Mean?
15. This is a literal statement. Father Joseph bought fruit and made his own preserves or jelly for breakfast.
16. See note 14 above.

Chapter 11: The Theology of Liberation
17. The phrase in French is *ayant son casse-croute dans sa poche*, literally "with a snack stashed away in his pocket."
18. See note 14 above.

Chapter 12: The Consecrated Life

19. Mendicant orders arose in the twelfth century with Saint Francis of Assisi. These religious went from door to door asking for alms; thus they were "mendicants"—beggars, from the Latin *mendicare* (to beg).

Other Books by Father Joseph Wresinski

Chronic Poverty and Lack of Basic Security: The Wresinski Report. 1994 (tr); 112 pages; $10.00. The English translation of this groundbreaking work, written for the Social and Economic Council of France. The Wresinski Report proposes an entirely new approach to fighting poverty based on partnership with the poorest themselves. It inspired new social policies in France, led to several United Nations resolutions, and continues to be studied by many countries and international bodies.

The Very Poor, Living Proof of the Indivisibility of Human Rights. 1994 (tr); 48 pages; $5.00. Father Joseph Wresinski's contribution to a fundamental review of human rights by the French National Advisory Committee on Human Rights.

Blessed Are You the Poor. 1992 (tr); 288 pages; $14.00. A fresh, revealing reading of the gospel with the very poor and through their eyes. This book leads the reader to better see the poorest people today and in the past, and to recognize what they can contribute to the world.

Other Books by the Fourth World Movement

Artisans of Democracy: How Ordinary People, Families in Extreme Poverty, and Social Institutions Become Allies to Overcome Social Exclusion. Jona M. Rosenfeld and Bruno Tardieu. 2000; 300 pages; $25.00. Published by University Press of America.

Reaching the Poorest. 1999; 124 pages; $10.00. Co-authored by the International Movement ATD Fourth World and UNICEF, this book presents seven case studies on the question: "How can the poorest people fully participate in the development of their countries and their communities?"

Extreme Poverty, The New Face of Apartheid. 1998; 35 pages; $2.00. Selected articles on extreme poverty and human rights. Translated from the Fourth World Movement's quarterly "Revue Quart Monde" of December 1998. Photocopy.

"As Good As Anyone," Martin Luther King Jr. 1997; 53 pages; $4.00. By Tapori children, New Orleans.

Talk With Us, Not At Us. 1996; 64 pages; $5.00. This book explores the concept of partnership between disadvantaged families in Great Britain and those from the legal, health, social, and community work professions who seek to work with them.

Father Joseph Wresinski: Voice of the Poorest. Alwine de Vos van Steenwijk. 1996; 200 pages; $8.95. The first biography of Father Joseph Wresinski. Recounts the life and thinking of the founder of the Fourth World Movement. Published by Queenship Publishing Company.

This Is How We Live. 1995; 172 pages; second edition; $12.00. Family histories from five continents form the basis for a discussion of key elements for better family policies.

The Family Album. 1994; 160 pages; $25.00. A collection of photographs, artwork, and texts in five languages, showing the reality and harshness of poverty throughout the world, but also the hope maintained against great odds through creativity, love, and friendship.

The Wresinski Approach: The Poorest—Partners in Democracy. 1991; 60 pages; $10.00. Representatives of the poorest families in Great Britain ask that their experience of poverty and their efforts to overcome it be taken as the starting point in anti-poverty initiatives.

The Human Face of Poverty. Vincent Fanelli. 1990; 144 pages; $12.50. A history of the first fifteen years of the Fourth World Movement's involvement with some of the poorest families in New York City. Published by Bootstrap Press.

Emergence From Extreme Poverty. Jona Rosenfeld. 1989; 110 pages; $9.50. An analysis of the Fourth World Movement's work and a description of the partnership between full-time volunteers and families in situations of extreme poverty.

Tapori Minibooks: True stories of children of courage. $1.00 each. Published in French, Spanish, and English. Eight different titles available.

To order these books, please contact:

Fourth World Movement USA
National Center
7600 Willow Hill Drive
Landover, MD 20785-4658
(301) 336-9489
www.atd-fourthworld.org

Of Related Interest

Catholic Social Teaching and Movements
Marvin Krier Mich

Putting human faces on the church's social teachings: that's what this unique book is about. The author aims to tell the story of Catholic social tradition from the perspective of the official teachings and the movements and persons that expressed and shaped that teaching.
0-89622-936-X, 488 pp, $29.95 (J-06)

Global Population from a Catholic Perspective
John C. Schwarz

This book surveys the complex issues involved in shaping population policies in the light of official church statements, the church's role in the United Nations, basic principles and new emphases in moral theology, and the role of the church in the modern world.
0-89622-932-7, 264 pp, $19.95 (J-03)

Religion, Ethics & the Common Good
James Donahue & M. Theresa Moser, RSCJ, editors

Sixteen members of the College Theology Society contribute essays covering a wide range of perspectives on some of today's most crucial theological questions, eg., "What is the common good?" "What are individual rights?" and "What role does the church and its theology have in addressing these issues?"
0-89622-701-4, 272 pp, $14.95 (M-78)

Liberation Theologies
The Global Pursuit of Justice
Alfred T. Hennelly, SJ

Surveys the ideas and ideals of the major players in the field of liberation theology, demonstrating the far-reaching implications of the principles involved.
0-89622-647-6, 392 pp, $19.95 (M-69)

Available at religious bookstores or from:

TWENTY-THIRD PUBLICATIONS
A Division of Bayard PO BOX 180 • MYSTIC, CT 06355
1-800-321-0411 • FAX: 1-800-572-0788 • E-MAIL: ttpubs@aol.com
www.twentythirdpublications.com
Call for a free catalog